Say It Again
For The Ones On The Front Row

Dennis L Taylor

Copyright © 2023 Dennis L Taylor

All rights reserved. No part of this book may be used or reproduced by any means, graphic, electronic, or mechanical, including photocopying, recording, taping, or by any information storage retrieval system without the written permission of the publisher except in the case of brief quotations embodied in critical articles and reviews.

Scriptures are taken from the New International Version of the Bible

Books may be ordered through booksellers or by contacting:
Dennis Taylor
luke252.dennis@gmail.com

RSIP
Raising the Standard International Publishing L. L. C.

ISBN: 9781960641045
Printed in the United States of America
Edition Date: May 2023

Contents

	Introduction	1
Chapter 1	Overcome Complacency	3
Chapter 2	A God-Sized Need	11
Chapter 3	A Vibrant Faith	20
Chapter 4	Plow The Fields	28
Chapter 5	Catch A Vision	37
Chapter 6	Refreshing	43
Chapter 7	A New Thing	51
Chapter 8	Stay Focused	62
Chapter 9	From Existing To Really Living	70
Chapter 10	Take Another Look	78
Chapter 11	Committed	81
Chapter 12	Compassion	87
Chapter 13	Where's The Zeal	94
Chapter 14	Doing Life Together	100
Chapter 15	Ready, Set, Go	105
	About The Author	111
	More Books By Dennis L Taylor	113

Introduction

I wanted to write a book encouraging the Church of Jesus Christ. I grew up in the Church and have seen many crazy things happen in business meetings on Sunday nights. Getting off track of what God has called us to be is so easy. We lose focus of our relationship with Jesus and become more concerned with position, power, and who gets the best solo at Christmas. We get stuck in our spiritual rut, and our spiritual vision gets cloudy. Then we find ourselves getting so busy, distracted, and overwhelmed with life that our relationship with God is on the back burner. Then it becomes easier to stray from what God called us to do.

There is nothing you will read in this book that you haven't heard before, but it needs to be repeated. I want to encourage the Church to overcome complacency, stay focused, be committed, and do body-life together. There is a huge God-sized need to reach the people around us with the Gospel of Jesus Christ. It is time to be refreshed, restored, and committed to the things of the Lord. "Refresh us, Lord, do a new thing within us and bring us from existing to really living."

It never hurts to hear the truth over again. Not only do we need to repeat it, but we need to say it a little louder too. We all need a little bit of encouragement along the way, especially when it comes to Christian ministry.

I pray that God will use these simple words to stir up a new passion in you, fueling you to keep spreading the Good News of Jesus Christ. This book is for those sitting in the front row, not necessarily for those who come occasionally. I pray this book will spark a fire in your heart and give you freshness in your walk with the Lord. To God be the glory forever and ever. *Say It Again*.

-1-
Overcoming Complacency

Amos 6:1: "Woe to you who are complacent in Zion, and to you who feel secure on Mount Samaria, you notable men of the foremost nation, to whom the people of Israel come!"

Have you eaten a massive meal of your favorite foods? Then you push away from the table and find a comfortable chair to watch a few minutes of TV. You get comfortable, and your eyes become heavy; before you know it, you are dead asleep. You are as content as you can be.

The same happens to us spiritually as believers in Jesus Christ, we get comfortable, satisfied, and lazy, and before we know it, we have fallen asleep. Then complacency settles in, and we are going through the motions of doing church. Before long, our relationship with Christ becomes just another relationship. Nothing special. We need to realize that relationships are doing one of two things. They are either growing or dying and to say a relationship is at a standstill is to believe a lie because a relationship is constantly changing.

Have you ever commented to a friend you haven't seen in a long time and said, "You haven't changed a bit?" Either you are lying, or you are being deceived. I guarantee you will see changes if you pull out an old picture from the past. We change so slowly; we don't notice the difference. Relationships are also constantly evolving. However, they are changing so slowly that we don't see the change.

Have you ever said, "My walk with Christ is fine; it is doing good? It's nothing to jump up and down about; it's ok." I think we all have been there and done that. But I want you to think about a time when you were the closest to God. Do you know that time in your life when you heard God's voice daily? That time in your life when the Word of God jumped off the page, or when you were so excited about ministry and going to church? Yes, that time in your life when you were full of passion and longed for the presence of God.

Where are you now in your spiritual walk with Jesus? I encourage you to stop and look honestly at your walk with Christ. Please don't fear taking a spiritual evaluation or calling it a spiritual checkup. Then you might be able to see how far you have wandered from the Lord. What happened? How did I get to this point? The change happened so slowly that we didn't even notice the difference. Wouldn't it be great to say, "Right now, I am closer to God than I've ever been, and I am seeking God's heart and will for my life?"

Suppose we could just let down that wall of pride that builds up over time. We could take off the mask and stop pretending we are good. To be honest with ourselves and be honest with God. As you know, that is hard to walk out. So how can we, as Children of God, avoid the relationship that should be essential in our life? God is calling us to be extraordinary. He is calling us to be different, and He is calling us to stand up and be counted. He is calling us to commit and to be sold out.

But what breaks the heart of God is when we choose to follow the crowd and live a lifestyle called casual Christianity. We are nothing extraordinary, just simple.

Say It Again

Have you ever wondered what causes us to live this lifestyle where we want to follow the crowd?

There are three things I want to bring up to make us aware of our drowsiness when it comes to our walk with Christ and how we minister to others outside the Church.

1. The Church of Jesus Christ has become complacent.

We have become satisfied and comfortable. We have come to a place in our relationship with Jesus where we tell God, "We're stopping right here, and we're not going to budge from our spot." Our spot is comfortable, we can handle it here, and we don't have to depend on God if we stay in our comfort zone. Complacency will blind us to how things should be and cause us to get a distorted picture of things. Is your relationship with God growing or dying?

> *Hosea 13:4-6: "But I am the Lord your God, who brought you out of Egypt. You shall acknowledge no God but me; I cared for you in the desert, in the land of burning heat. When I fed them, they were satisfied; when they were satisfied, they became proud; then they forgot me."*

God reminded Israel of all that He had done for Israel. He cared for them in the desert. He provided food when they were hungry, and He fed them. Then when God fed them and provided for them as a nation, they quickly became satisfied and forgot who blessed them. When we become comfortable, we can become very proud and complacent. We all are so guilty of doing the same thing in our lives. Sometimes we reach the point of need and cry to God, and He responds in grace. Once our needs are met, our hunger for God stops. Then another brick is added to the wall of pride in our life.

2. We become carnal.

> *1 Corinthians 3:1-3a: "Brothers, I could not address you as spiritual but as worldly-mere infants in Christ. I gave you milk, not solid food, for you were not yet ready. You are still worldly."*

In other words, the Church can easily slide into worldliness, materialism, and wanting to do everything our way. Carnality and worldliness hinder our ability to grow in Christ. That attitude is also known as sin, which blocks our communication with the Lord. God, our Father, has so much to show and tell us, but we have become men and women of this world. We have allowed the love of money, wealth, power, and position to consume our passion and thoughts. These things have become more important to us than our passion for God and His work.

3. We enjoy what is comfortable.

Don't you love those feel-good sermons? We love hearing how good we are doing and those sermons giving us that warm and fuzzy feeling. But what about those sermons that are stepping on our toes? It is almost like the pastor knows our whole story and is preaching right at us. God has a way of shining the spotlight on our sins and selfishness. I have learned over the years that we can run from God but will never outrun Him. So, why even try? If we are in the right standing with the Lord, no sermon will make us uncomfortable. Not many of us like to get outside our comfort zones and don't like it when we seem way over our heads. So we decided to play it safe, splash around in the kiddie pool of faith, and never get into the deep water. We want to do what we have always done rather than trusting God to do something fresh and new. Churches are full of comfortable Christians. They have no desire to grow, and they want to stay right where they are in their relationship with God. Because they only want to do what is safe and know they can handle it with their strength and wisdom. Has our faith become a faith of convenience and comfort?

Think about it this way, was Jesus about convenience or comfort? No, Jesus was fully committed. He was all in! Jesus willingly received a crown of thorns. He took all the humiliation and suffering that was meant for us. Our Lord allowed people to spit in his face and be nailed on an old rugged cross. He willingly took my place and suffered, bled, and died. That didn't sound like a life of comfort to me.

Casual Christianity is a lifestyle that doesn't please God. It's a self-centered lifestyle that doesn't attract the lost to a saving relationship with Jesus. So, how do we escape it? Is there hope? There is hope, and we can overcome it. Not because of our strength and wisdom but because Christ lives in us, the hope of all glory.

We must first remind ourselves how much He loved us to overcome complacency. Then, we must take our eyes off ourselves and reflect on what Christ has done for us. Imagine yourself about to be hung on a nasty cross; soldiers are holding you down where another soldier could drive a nail in your hands and feet. Can you imagine the fear and the terror raging through your mind and spirit? After facing the pain and suffering, you face eternity with no hope. Then Jesus steps up, freeing you from the soldiers' grasp, and willingly takes your place. See the pain on His face, the blood dripping down His temples, and His fists grasped tightly. What an amazing love the Father has for us.

> Romans 5:6-8: *"You see, at just the right time, when we were still powerless, Christ died for the ungodly. Very rarely will anyone die for a righteous, though for a good man, someone might dare to die. But God demonstrates his love for us in this: While we were still sinners, Christ died for us."*

If that wasn't enough, consider what He saved us from. He loved us enough to remove the dirtiness of our sins through His precious blood. He helps us to overcome sin and the guilt to flood our minds and spirit. He gives us hope when there seems to be no way to overcome an obstacle. For those in Christ, He has provided an eternal home with no pain, suffering, or more struggles. What a day of rejoicing that will be when we all see Jesus.

To overcome complacency, we must not only remind ourselves how much He loved us, but we must also remember that commitment we made to Him when we received Him as Savior. Do you recall that day when you said yes to Jesus? Do you remember that day when you said, "I surrender all?" It was the greatest decision I would ever make in my life. Something happened that day that would change my life forever. That day, I committed my life to follow Jesus no matter the cost. This decision was a life-long covenant with the Lord that I would spend my entire life following His lead no matter what. That day we received Christ, we all committed to die to ourselves. We committed to doing what He thought was best. We decided to lay down our rights and will to serve Him and His Church.

The third thing we all need to do to overcome the spirit of complacency is fully submit to the Lord and come near to God. In other words, we must pursue a love relationship with the Father more than anything else.

> *James: 4:7-9: "Submit yourselves, then, to God. Resist the devil, and he will flee from you. Come near to God, and he will come near to you. Wash your hands, you sinners, and purify your hearts, you double-minded. Grieve, mourn, and wail. Change your laughter to mourning and your joy to gloom. Humble yourselves before the Lord, and he will lift you up."*

There comes a time in our Christian faith when we must be honest before God. First, we must swallow our pride and come boldly before His throne of grace. Then we must submit our entire being to our Heavenly Father and hold nothing back. This faith encounter is our all-in moment. Flee Satan's traps and temptations and pursue God with everything you have. Realize we are not here to grow a church or a Sunday School class. It is not to make you look good in your community but to pursue God for His glory. There needs to be a time for confession and repentance. He wants to hear it from you. Hold nothing back and allow God to work in your heart and soul.

Don't settle for complacency, carnal ways, or what's comfortable or convenient. Christ asks us to seek Him with everything we have and be willing to give Him our very best. His call to His Church is to hold nothing back and walk out a life that will make Him smile. It's time to stop playing the game of church. It's time to get our priorities straight and put our focus back on Jesus Christ. Don't be scared to ask God for an unquenchable hunger for the Word of God. Ask Him to give you a burden for those who do not know Jesus as Lord and Savior. We, the church, need to get out of our spiritual Lazy-Boy recliners and wake up spiritually. It's time to turn the world upside down for the glory of Christ. Let's sound the alarm and encourage each other to compete for the prize of Christ. We can't be satisfied with the crumbs on the carpet, and we can't be happy with the status quo.

> *1 Thessalonians 5:17: "Therefore encourage one another and build each other up, just as in fact you are doing."*

Overcome complacency by reflecting on God's great love for us and remembering what we committed to the Lord the day we received Him as Lord and Savior. Then fully submit to His will and chase after Him with everything you have. Sound the alarm, Church; we have a mission to complete.

-2-
A God-Sized Need

Have you ever had a God-sized need? Have you ever wondered how you were going to overcome a difficult situation? If you haven't, get ready because it is coming. It is just a matter of time. Things in life will knock you to your knees and leave your world spinning.

What is a God-sized need anyway? It's a need that comes to us whether we like it or not. It's a need that overwhelms us because we have no idea how to handle or overcome the difficulty. It's a need that we can't pay back or even understand why we have to face something so complex. Seeing this kind of need shows me I am not enough. I am not smart enough. I am not rich enough. I am not wise enough to find a solution to make things right. But I serve a God who can. I serve a God who has the answer to all of life's difficulties and problems. He is the great I Am. He is able. He is in total control.

I confess this to you today, the closer I get to my Heavenly Father, the more He amazes me. My God is still in the miracle-working business and moves mountains daily. Therefore, we should not be surprised when God shows up to meet a God-Sized need. On the contrary, we should be anticipating it.

The Church of Jesus Christ has a God-Sized need today. We have a mission that Jesus gave us in Matthew 28:18-20:

> *"All authority in heaven and on earth has been given to me. Therefore, go and make disciples of all*

nations, baptizing them in the name of the Father and of the Son and of the Holy Spirit, and teaching them to obey everything I have commanded you. And surely I am with you always, to the very end of the age."

As the Church of Jesus Christ, we have a huge God-sized need. Jesus called us to spread the Gospel of Jesus Christ worldwide, mentoring and teaching them to obey and follow everything God has commanded. We have a God-sized need because we are taught to love each other regardless of circumstances. With so many different types of people living around us, loving unconditionally is becoming harder and harder. So many people do not think the way we think. We live and walk among people who grow up in different environments and are raised differently from us. However, God calls us to love one another despite our differences. That in itself is a God-sized need to love those around us day in and day out. Does God's mission for His Church overwhelm you? Does His call to believers cause you anxiety and stress? People worldwide need to hear about the Gospel of Jesus Christ. That is a God-sized need.

The Bible is full of God-sized needs. What about Daniel in the lion's den? Think about it. God didn't save Daniel from the lion's den; He saved him in the lion's den. What about Shadrach, Meshach, and Abednego? King Nebuchadnezzar had these men of God thrown into a fiery furnace, and it looked like they were about to lose their lives. They had a God-sized need. There was no way out, and everything seemed hopeless. But somehow, these three men of God were in perfect peace. What about the children of Israel when they were running from Pharaoh and his army? They were caught between a rock and a hard place. Pharaoh's army pressed them from behind, and the Red Sea blocked their way to freedom. The children of Israel needed a miracle because they were in an impossible situation. They all had a God-sized need, but they all had hope.

Did God come through? He sure did. I am not going to act like Moses didn't feel the pressure of Pharaoh coming behind him, and I am not going to say Moses didn't have his doubts. I am sure Moses struggled and possibly questioned God's faithfulness. Sometimes it takes God-sized needs to get us back on track and remember who is in control. In those God-sized needs, we will discover that we must come to a place where we depend on Christ. Those difficult times help us discover what we believe about God and our faith in Him.

In Matthew 14:15-21, Jesus was teaching and healing the sick, and then we find another God-sized need that was placed in front of the disciples:

> *"As evening approached, the disciples came to him and said, 'This is a remote place, and it's already getting late. Send the crowds away, so they can go to the villages and buy themselves some food.' Jesus replied, 'They do not need to go away. You give them something to eat.' We have only five loaves of bread and two fish,' they answered. 'Bring them here to me,' he said. And he directed the people to sit down on the grass. Taking the five loaves and the two fish and looking up to heaven, he gave thanks and broke the loaves. Then he gave them to the disciples, and the disciples gave them to the people. They all ate and were satisfied, and the disciples picked up twelve basketfuls of broken pieces that were left over. The number of those who ate was about five thousand men, besides women and children."*

What an amazing example of Jesus meeting a God-sized need. Could Jesus have made the fish and the bread appear before each family without using the disciples to distribute the food? I believe he could have done that, without a doubt. But Jesus required something of the disciples that day that He also requires of us in our day-to-day life. Look again at verses 17 and 18, when Jesus asked his disciples to bring the bread and fish to Him. Jesus required obedience from His disciples. Think about it; the disciples could have made excuses why this could be a waste of their time. Or rationalized in their minds and questioned Jesus and what He was thinking. Don't you know that the disciples had to be thinking, what is Jesus up to, and what will He do with these five loaves and two fish? Yet, they were obedient. They brought the bread and the fish to Jesus. This request probably didn't make sense to the disciples, but that didn't stop them from obeying Jesus.

As the Church of Jesus Christ, we must obey our Heavenly Father. Yet, at times, if we were honest with each other, we don't know precisely how God will work out those God-sized needs in our lives. I am talking about those times when all hope is gone, and you need a miracle from God. I am talking about those times when you have tried everything, and nothing seems to change the situation. Yes, when you cry out to God, He doesn't respond. Yet, God still calls us to hear His voice and obey.

Look at how Isaiah responded when he received a vision from God in Isaiah 6:8:

> *"Then I heard the voice of the saying, 'Whom shall I send? And who will go for us?' And I said. 'Here am I. Send me!'"*

Say It Again

When God-sized needs come, be willing to be obedient even if it doesn't make sense; instead of being overwhelmed or running around frantically trying to come up with a solution or find a way out of this difficulty. Turn to the Lord and trust Him. I know that is easier said than done. But speaking from experience, my great idea or reasoning tends to worsen the situation, and I find myself in a deeper hole. Can we follow Isaiah's example and say to the Lord in difficult situations, "Here am I, send me."

When we finally follow Christ in complete obedience, take a guess what God will ask of us next. Right out of the gate, He will call us to serve. Sometimes that is the last thing we want to do because that sounds like too much work. Yet, our society today wants to be served. Our culture tells us to look out for number one and not let anyone run us over. O how the Church of Jesus Christ needs a sense of humility and compassion for the world around us. But with that call to service, God will open the doors for us to work to build His Kingdom. Does that word "work" scare you away? Maybe you think I work enough already. You may work eight to ten hours a day to earn a living. Then I come home and clean the house, wash clothes, and mow the lawn. Why would you need more work to be placed in my crazy life?

Place yourself in the disciple's shoes when Jesus asks them to bring him the five loaves of bread and the two fish. After they obeyed Jesus, He asked them to serve the people—approximately 15,000 people with women and children. Now keep in mind that these were mostly church people. It's sad to say, but it's probably the truth. A recent study was taken, and this study asked waiters and waitresses what day is the most difficult to work. Most of them said Sunday. When asked why Sunday, they responded and said, "When the church people get out of the church, they usually come in a hurry to be seated and serve. They usually come in bigger groups, are more demanding, and tip the least. Now with all that in mind, can you get a picture of the disciples hustling around serving bread and fish to everyone? Can you see Paul getting aggravated with all the kids running around and not listening to what the parents say? So many people to feed and not enough people to serve, and the disciples are wide open, doing their best. Now is that hitting home with any church leaders? Can you see Jesus breaking the bread, blessing it, and watching the disciple hand out all the food? I can see Jesus looking at the disciples, shaking his head, and saying, "They have so much to learn."

The disciples obeyed Jesus, and they were willing to serve. Because of their obedience and willingness to help, Jesus met a God-sized need, and there were plenty of leftovers. What seemed impossible for the disciples even to imagine became possible because of Jesus' willingness to bless. I guarantee you this task wasn't easy, and it was probably aggravating at times, but seeing the mighty work of Jesus made it all worth it.

> *Matthew 14:22-30: "Immediately Jesus made the disciples get into the boat and go on ahead of him to the other side, while he dismissed the crowd. After he dismissed them, he went up to a mountainside by himself to pray. When the evening came, he was there alone, but the boat was already a considerable distance from land, buffeted by the waves because the wind was against it. During the fourth watch of the night Jesus went out to them, walking on the lake. When the disciples saw him walking on the lake, they were terrified. 'It is a ghost,' they said and cried out in fear. But Jesus immediately said to them: 'Take*

Say It Again

courage! It is I. Don't be afraid.' 'Lord, if it's you,' Peter replied, 'tell me to come to you on the water.' 'Come,' he said. Then Peter got down out of the boat, walked on water, and came toward Jesus. But when he saw the wind, he was afraid and, beginning to sink, cried out, 'Lord, save me!'"

After this great miracle, Jesus placed his disciples in a boat and sent them to the other side. Then Jesus sent the crowd home with a full belly; then he went to the mountainside to pray alone. While Jesus was praying, the disciples found themselves in a storm. This storm had to be pretty rough. Don't forget that a few of the disciples were professional fishermen, and some had been in storms before. But this storm was different. They were all afraid. Have you ever noticed that difficult situations always seem to pop up after a miracle or a mighty move of God? Think about it; the disciple experienced a miracle of Jesus. They had served all day and were so tired that they wanted to sit down and rest. Then Jesus sent them to the other side of the lake. Now place yourselves in the disciple's shoes. You are tired, and your feet are killing you from waiting on fifteen thousand people. Now, Jesus is asking us to row across the vast lake. Then a storm comes in the middle of the night, and you are scared. What else could go wrong? Can you see these men in this boat? Can you imagine the emotion and their fear level? If that wasn't enough to rattle them, Jesus came walking across the water. That pushed the disciples over the edge, and their hearts sunk in great fear.

Thank goodness, Jesus identified himself and told the disciples to fear not. Of course, one of the disciples spoke up. You guessed it; it was Peter. He always seemed to have something to say. Peter said to Jesus, "If that is you, bid me to come to you on the water." Can you see all the other disciples thinking about why Peter always has to be the center of attention? But to their surprise, Jesus responded to Peter by saying, "Come." In other words, Jesus said, "Get out of the boat and come to me! Another way to say it is; Get out of your comfort zone and step out on faith. Come to a point in your life where you must depend on me. Jesus asked Peter to place himself where he wasn't in control, and his wisdom was insufficient. Step out of your safe boat and trust me with your life. Can you see Peter gripping the side of the boat, and can you imagine the fear that filled his soul? His heart had to be racing, and so many thoughts ran through his mind. But Peter lets go of the side of the boat and begins to walk to Jesus.

As a believer in Jesus, have you experienced a miracle of God? Maybe a gift of a changed life of someone close to you, or it may be a radical move of God in your church home. Things are going so well, then a life storm hits and knocks us for a loop. If we are honest with ourselves and God, we are tired and worn out. We need to rest, but this difficult issue has popped up. How are you going to handle it? Will we shrink back in fear, or will we let go of the side of the boat and walk to Jesus? Will we trust God and lean into Him and His strength? There is no greater joy or excitement than doing something Christ has asked you to do, knowing you couldn't do it alone. Peter experienced the power of God.

In verse thirty, Peter saw the wind and the waves and began to sink. What happened? He took his eyes off Jesus. We all could give Peter a hard time and get on him for the lack of faith, but we need to give him some credit. Think about it, how many of the disciples walked on water? One! The other eleven stayed on the boat. Jesus reached out to Peter, pulled him out of the water, and walked him back to

Say It Again

the boat. I will guarantee you one thing; Peter will never forget that day. That day He taught Peter who was in control and Lord over all.

Let me try and wrap this chapter up. As Christians, we must be obedient when we face a God-sized need. In other words, we have to be willing to say. "Lord, I commit everything I have to you. No more holding back and resisting. No turning back." You better prepare to serve when we surrender it all to the King. Swallow selfish pride and humble yourself before almighty God. I don't care who gets the credit for all your hard work. Then get ready to get busy for the glory of God. Just like Peter, make sure you keep your eyes on Jesus Christ. Make that love relationship with Jesus your top priority, and He will give us what we need to overcome any situation.

-3-
A Vibrant Faith

Suppose I were to sit a hot cup of freshly brewed coffee in front of you. Then I placed another cup of coffee that had been poured for about an hour and had become lukewarm; which would you choose? Before you give me your answer, I want to provide you with another situation to think about. Please work with me here; this will take a little time. I want to get you thinking. Now imagine you are trying to spruce up your home, and you want to give it some color and life. You have friends coming over and want to make your home feel inviting. My question is, will you choose the fresh-cut flowers that are bright and alive, or do you decide to go with flowers that have been cut for days, the color has faded, and are beginning to wither? Of course, you will choose the hot cup of coffee and the freshly cut flowers. You would make these choices because we prefer fresh and vibrant over stale and dull any day.

If that is true of coffee and flowers, why do believers settle for a stale, used faith when we can have a fresh, vibrant, and growing faith? Why settle for second best? Why not thrive instead of just getting by? I want to share four encouragements that can help you keep your faith vibrant and growing. Please pray through these four challenges and push through those tough, dry times that always seem to come to us.

First, I challenge you to keep your faith fresh as an individual and a church.

Joshua 24:14-15; 31 says, "Now fear the Lord and serve him with all faithfulness. Throw away the gods

Say It Again

your forefathers worshiped beyond the River and in Egypt, and serve the Lord. But if serving the Lord seems undesirable to you, choose for yourselves this day whom you will serve, whether the gods your forefathers served beyond the River or the gods of the Amorites, in whose land you are living. But as for me and my household, we will serve the Lord."

Who is that person in your life that has challenged you spiritually to grow in Christ? Make sure to come up with at least one person who has mentored and pushed you in your relationship with Christ. Send a text or an encouraging email to thank them for their efforts and prayers. Now describe how you would describe a vibrant faith. Once you have a clear picture of deep faith, I want to ask you a fundamental question. Do you have that kind of faith? That can be a tricky question to answer. So, how do we keep ourselves fresh? We must first serve Him with all faithfulness. Yes, that means our church attendance, our Bible reading, our prayer time, and even sharing our faith. Then, we must return to the basics and make it more about our love relationship with Jesus. We must also put away all other gods! What idols have we allowed to take over the thrones of our hearts? Is it money or saving up for retirement? Is it the love of sports or following your favorite football team? The scripture that we just read in Joshua challenged us to choose this day whom we serve. Joshua made it clear whom he was serving. There were no mixed emotions or no time for being wishy-washy. Where do you stand? What do you believe? Faith involves us making a decision. No one drifts into a vibrant love relationship with Jesus. It takes time, effort, energy, and commitment. A deep faith also involves the family. How powerful is it when you see an entire household serving God and loving on people around them?

In most cases (not all), as the father goes, so goes the family. Keep that faith fresh, and ask God to renew your steadfast spirit. Ask Him to restore the joy of your salvation. You will be surprised how powerful a few short prayers can be.

Look at David's prayer that he prayed to His Heavenly Father in Psalm 51:10-12:

> *"Create in me a pure heart, O God, and renew a steadfast spirit within me. Do not cast me from your presence or take your Holy Spirit from me. Restore to me the joy of your salvation and grant me a willing spirit, to sustain me."*

What an awesome short prayer to pray for a vibrant faith. God loves to hear us pray. He loves to listen to words that we speak from our hearts. He loves to hear simple, heartfelt confessions to Him. Keep your faith fresh.

The second thing I want to challenge you to do is to demonstrate a fully obedient faith.

> *Judges 1:1;8: "After the death of Joshua, the Israelites asked the Lord, 'Who will be the first to go up and fight for us against the Canaanites?' When Israel became strong, they pressed the Canaanites into forced labor but never drove them out completely."*

Joshua died, and Israel began compromising what God had told them to do. They were to entirely drive out the Canaanites from the land but didn't fully obey what the Lord told them to do. We sometimes reason why we don't

Say It Again

listen to what God tells us. We can make all kinds of excuses and reason in our heads why our way of thinking is ok. Let's call it what it is; it is disobedience to God. They allowed the Canaanites to stay in the land for cheap labor. We live in disobedience when we don't fully obey what God tells us. Know this; God doesn't bless disobedience. Israel became more interested in their economic well-being than their walk with the Lord. In other words, they compromised their faith.

God is looking for someone willing to obey Him no matter the cost. He is looking for a Church willing to do what He tells them to do. What about you? Are you taking time to listen to your Heavenly Father? Are you fully committed to the call of God, and are you willing to obey His voice? Keep your faith fresh and demonstrate a fully obedient faith.

If we maintain a vibrate faith, we must reject substitutes for faith in the Lord.

> *Judges 2:10-12: "After that whole generation had been gathered to their fathers, and another generation grew up, who knew neither the Lord nor what he had done for Israel. Then the Israelites did evil in the eyes of the Lord and served the Baals. They forsook the Lord, the God of their fathers, who brought them out of Egypt. They followed and worshiped various gods of the people around them. They provoke the Lord to anger."*

When the Church of Jesus Christ begins to stray from God, we begin to find substitutes for God. As in Israel's case, they turned to Baal and other gods. They forgot God, and they compromised their faith. Our compromised faith often hinders our children and others we may influence. Look what happens in the following verses as a result of Israel finding substitutes for God in Judges 2:13-15:

> *"Because they forsook him and served Baal and the Ashtoreths. In his anger against Israel, the Lord handed them over to raiders who plundered them. He sold them to their enemies all around, whom they were no longer able to resist. Whenever Israel went out to fight, the hand of the Lord was against them to defeat them, just as he had sworn to them. They were in great distress."*

Is your life or you're the life of your church in great distress? Are there things in your life that have become more important than your relationship with God? Before we move on, is there a sin you need to confess? Is there something you need to get right with the Lord? Are there priorities that need to be adjusted or reworked? Then, have the guts to confess it to the Lord.

Let's review before we get to the last challenge. To keep our faith growing, we must keep our faith fresh. We must demonstrate a fully obedient faith and reject any substitutes for faith in Jesus Christ.

Last but not least, we must go after a mature faith.

> *1 Corinthians 3:1-3: "Brothers, I could not address you as spiritual but as worldly, mere infants in Christ. I gave you milk, not solid food, for you were not yet ready. Indeed, you are still not ready. You are still worldly. For since there is jealousy and quarreling among you, are you not worldly? Are you not acting like mere men?"*

Say It Again

Can you sense the frustration in Paul's words as he writes this letter to the Church in Corinth? I know Paul wanted to see the Church grow and flourish in faith, but they seemed to struggle with the maturity level of their trust. Paul desired that they would eat spiritual steak and potatoes but was still sipping on spiritual baby formula. It's time believers consider where we stand in our walk with Jesus Christ. Slow down enough to take a spiritual evaluation and ask yourself some tough questions. How would you respond if I asked you how your time alone with God is going? What would you say? For most Christians, they would say it's nonexistent, or it's ok. Nothing to jump up and down about. Take a look at what Jesus said to the Church of Sardis in Revelation 3:1-3:

> *"I know your deeds; you have a reputation of being alive, but you are dead. Wake up! Strengthen what remains and is about to die, for I have not found your deeds complete in the sight of my God. Remember, therefore, what you have received and heard; obey it, and repent. But if you do not wake up, I will come like a thief, and you will not know at what time I will come to you."*

I will not get deep into this, but I want to touch on five things to do if you're going to mature in your faith. Let's make this as simple as possible.

1. Wake up! Wake up from your spiritual slumber.

I must move and get out of that comfortable bed to wake up in the morning. I have to get my coffee and walk around. The same is true regarding our spiritual slumber; we must get up and move from our comfortable spot. I am not telling you to move from your residence, but you must be willing to progress spiritually. It may be uncomfortable or scary, but you will survive.

2. Strengthen what remains.

Remind yourself of the gift that God has given you to share with others. Return to the promises God had written on your heart's door and rekindle that fire barely burning in your soul. Get back to that spiritual gym and work out those muscles in Christ that need to be worked. You may be sore, but it will be worth it.

3. Remember what you have received and heard from the Lord over the years.

Take time to reflect on the goodness of God. Go back to the day you received Jesus as your Lord and Savior. Take time to thank Him for His faithfulness and His grace. Go back to the scriptures that spoke to your heart years ago. Embrace His Holy Word and soak in His presence. Ask the Lord to help you recall old dreams and passions that you once had when it came to your relationship with Him.

4. Obey it.

It's not enough to hear God; we must obey what God has put in our hearts. We need to walk it out. Let those dreams come alive in Christ. Hang on to the promises of God's Word. Don't give up or quit when obstacles or hard times come. Be willing to push through difficulty but be yoked with Christ. Please don't do it in your strength and wisdom.

Say It Again

5. Repent.

Get alone with God and get everything straight with your Heavenly Father. Confess your doubts, frustrations, and sins, and name them individually. Then, hold nothing back and leave it all on the throne of Jesus. He is faithful to forgive and cleanse us from all unrighteousness.

As believers in Jesus, we must settle for nothing less than a growing faith. We are called to gain spiritual maturity and become more like Christ in all that we do. Growing in our faith is like riding a bike; if we are not going forward, we will fall. It is time to strengthen the love relationship with Jesus Christ. It's time to put down our spiritual bottles and take off our spiritual diapers. It's time to move from that same spot you have been standing for years. That spot may be perfect. No doubt about it, but there is so much more to experience in Christ. Know this; His Word is fresh and new every day. There is an adventure around every corner if you open your heart and mind to the world's Savior. Your best life is right in front of you. Get into God's back pocket and enjoy the ride.

-4-
Plow The Fields

If you have ever studied church history, you know that often a church will be great in one generation and falter in the next. They sat on their blessing and got comfortable or refused to obey the Father. More than ever before, we, the church, need to seek His face and pray to our Father. It is time to draw close to Him and pray bolder prayers for the glory of Christ.

> *Matthew 9:35-38: "Jesus went through all the towns and villages, teaching in their synagogues, preaching the good news of the kingdom and healing every disease and sickness. When he saw the crowds, he had compassion on them because they were harassed and helpless, like a sheep without a shepherd. Then he said to his disciples, 'The harvest is plentiful but the workers are few. Ask the Lord of the harvest, therefore, to send out workers into his harvest field."*

Jesus made an impact; He engaged His community. Church, it's time to plow the fields and be obedient to the call of Christ. It's time to use our talents to reach a world that needs to hear good news and experience the life-giving grace of God. Do we share Jesus' heart and passion for others? Do we impact people around us daily? Do we go out of our way to encourage those down and out?

Let me start by asking you a few more questions. Please don't rush over these questions and continue to read, but take time to reflect and pray over each question. Think

Say It Again

through them and then write down your thoughts and reflections. Here we go. What do you weep about? In other words, what breaks your heart? I am not talking about when your favorite college football team loses. I am talking about the deep-rooted passion God has placed in your soul that causes you pain if it doesn't come through. What drives you or motivates you? What is that God-dream that God has placed in your life? Where is the passion in our ministry and Church? Take time to pause, pray, and reflect. I pray that God will stir up something in your heart that will bubble to the top of your attention. Then embrace what God has placed in you and run after it passionately. Allow your Heavenly Father to till the ground of your heart and get ready to see the harvest of God's work in your life.

One thing is for sure; we will never make an impact while in our comfort zone. I am not a farmer, but I know the fallow ground is unproductive and undisturbed. After the soil has broken up, rock and weeds must be removed. The tilling has to be deep for us to see a great harvest. The preparation is never easy, but necessary if we want to see a great harvest.

After Jesus departed, what if the disciples sat around and played 'remember when?' What if Billy Graham never shared what God placed in his heart? You see, God is looking for that one man, woman, and Church that would dare to be different. It is time to plow the fields. It is time to put into action what we believe. We must fight for our kids' and students' hearts and lives. They are not our future; they are our blessings now. We have to be willing to invest money, time, blood, sweat, and tears.

> *John 4:34-35: "My food," Jesus said, 'is to do the will of him who sent me and to finish his work. Do not say, 'Four months more, and then the harvest?' I tell you,*

open your eyes and look at the fields! They are ripe for harvest.'"

Are we, the Church, willing to storm the gates of hell to fight for our children? Are we willing to put ourselves out there to reach our students for Jesus Christ? Are we ready to risk our reputation to win others to Jesus? The Church of the Living God has to make an impact beyond the four walls of a church building. So it's sad to say, but sometimes the truth hurts. I have seen more fighting in the church than fighting against the real enemy. Rise up, Church! Let's put on the armor of God and meet Satan head-on. In Christ, we will overcome. In Christ, we will reach the heart and souls of people around us. Let's set aside our differences and link arms to share the Gospel of Jesus Christ with a lost and dying world. We must know whom we are fighting and learn how to fight them properly.

Do you know the difference between a donkey and a thoroughbred horse? It's how they respond when they feel threatened. Thoroughbreds will stand in a circle and face each other, then kick out their hind legs. Donkeys will stand facing the enemies with their backs to each other and kick each other to death. We need more thoroughbreds in the church who will storm the gates of hell and not kick each other in the process. Imagine what the Holy Spirit could do through us if we can set aside our pride and stubbornness. How many lives will be changed? How many marriages would be healed? How many people's minds would be set free? We can't settle for less than God's best.

Mark 5:25-34: "And a woman was there who had been subject to bleeding for twelve years. She had suffered a great deal under the care of many doctors and had spent all she had, yet instead of getting better, she grew worse. When she heard about Jesus, she came up behind him in the crowd and touched his cloak, because she thought, 'If I just touch his clothes, I will be healed.' Immediately her bleeding stopped and she felt in her body that she was freed from her suffering. At once Jesus realized that power had gone out from him. He turned around in the crowd and asked, 'Who touched my clothes?' 'You see the people crowding against you,' his disciples answered, 'and yet you can ask, 'Who touched me?' But Jesus kept looking around to see who had done it. Then the woman, knowing what had happened to her, came and fell at his feet and, trembling with fear, told him the whole truth. He said to her. 'Daughter, your faith has healed you. Go in peace and be freed from your suffering.'"

This woman had been suffering severely from an issue of blood. She tried everything to be healed and made whole. She went to every doctor in town and tried every home remedy. She was desperate. She had a ton of medical bills which left her broke. She had this incurable disease and no hope of getting better. She was marked as ceremonially unclean due to this issue of blood. But she possessed the kind of desperation that God was looking for. Not only was she desperate, but she was also willing to act in faith. Can you see her working her way through the crowd? All she wanted to do was get close to Jesus and touch the hem of his garments. She had confidence that Jesus could make her new. Throughout the Gospels, Jesus was attractive to desperate people.

Mark 2:1-5: "A few days later, when Jesus again entered Capernaum, the people heard that he had come home. So many gathered that there was no room left, not even outside the door, and he preached the word to them. Some men came, bringing to him a paralytic, carried by four of them. Since they could not get him to Jesus because of the crowd, they made an opening in the roof above Jesus and, after digging through it, lowered the mat the paralyzed man was lying on. When Jesus saw their faith, he said to the paralytic, 'Son, your sins are forgiven.'"

These men were desperate to get their friend to Jesus. Think about it, when they arrived at the home where Jesus was teaching and they saw the crowd, most of us would have turned around and gone back home. We would have reasoned and thought we would never get our friend to Jesus in this crazy crowd. They knew carrying this man through this crowd would have been impossible. So they devised a plan for what they had to do to get their friend to the top of this house. Don't you wish we had more details on how they got their friend to the roof of this house? I can imagine there was a story within a story. Four men can come up with some crazy solutions on the fly. Did they get two ladders and set them side by side, and two men strained to get him to the roof? They likely used rope to tie to this man's mat and pull him up.

Try to imagine their conversation. Again, these four men probably knew what would work best. Was there fussing about what would work best? Don't you know they are giving each other a hard time carrying their fair share of the load? Once they get their friend to the top of this house, imagine the noise they were making trying to bust through the roof. The owner had to be there and hear all the banging noises. Don't you think he excused himself to walk outside to see what was going on? Don't you think he was trying to stop these crazy guys from messing up his roof? These four

Say It Again

men had to know they would have to fix everything they tore up. They knew there would be a cost.

They finished busting through the roof, and they lowered their friend to the feet of Jesus. Have you ever wondered how Jesus responded to all the noise while teaching? Did he crack some jokes or use this odd experience to teach the truth on the fly? We may never know, but one thing is that Jesus was attractive to desperate people. These four men were willing to do whatever it took to get their friend to Jesus.

> Mark 10:46-52: "Then they came to Jericho. As Jesus and his disciples, together with a large crowd were leaving the city, a bling man Bartimaeus was sitting by the roadside begging. When he heard that it was Jesus of Nazareth, he began to shout, 'Jesus, Son of David, have mercy on me!' Many rebuked him and told him to be quiet, but he shouted all the more, 'Son of David, have mercy on me!' Jesus stopped and said, 'Call him.' So they called the blind man, 'Cheer up! On your feet! He's calling you.' Throwing his cloak aside, he jumped to his feet and came to Jesus. 'What do you want me to do for you?' Jesus asked him. The blind man said, 'Rabbi, I want to see.' 'Go,' said Jesus, 'your faith has healed you.' Immediately he received his sight and followed Jesus along the road."

Blind Bartimaeus pressed through the opposition. He could have given up when people told him to be quiet and to leave Jesus alone. But think about it; everyone wanted to see Jesus. Everyone wanted to be close to Him and have the privilege of talking with Him. So why would Jesus have time for this blind man? What would He stop to listen to his plea for his sight? But Jesus stopped! All the things that were on Jesus' agenda for that day, and he paused to heal this beggar that had nothing. Jesus was attracted to those who were desperate.

We must press through the obstacles and the opposition to get to Jesus. Unfortunately, too many churches and church leaders resemble the rich young ruler instead of blind Bartimaeus. We want life on our terms. We want the ministry to fit our schedule. We don't like to be inconvenienced by the cross of Christ. But listen to this truth: No church can make an impact until it is willing to get to Jesus, no matter the cost. If we lean on our understanding, we will only have a ministry of flesh, wood, hay, and stubble. We sit in our buildings and listen to the sermons, but are we just checking a box if we are not overwhelmed with urgency? One thing is for sure; the majority will never push for revival. Consider it: a movement of God is an inconvenient interruption for the status quo.

As the Church of Jesus Christ, we must pursue His presence and call on Him in prayer. First, we must fall on our faces and ask Him to send a revival and let it begin in us. Then we must be willing to get to Jesus no matter the cost, plow the fields, and plant the seeds of faith. Pray to the Heavenly Father to send the rain of His Glory. Send the rain of His love. Send the rain of His Holy Spirit! It's time for us to cry out to Jesus and not stop praying when things get complicated. Church, we must keep plowing even when it doesn't look like rain, even when you can't see a harvest.

I want to close this chapter and remind you that Satan will not sit back and watch you plow. He is the author of lies and deception. He wants to kill, steal, and destroy. He wants to cause as much damage as possible to the Church of Jesus

Say It Again

Christ. With that in mind, I want to give you three things to think about that will help you fight the good fight of faith.

1. Selfishness and pride have to go.

Relationships have to be restored. There has to be a time for a confession. Swallow that pride and go and make things right between God and those around you. Make sure to read Matthew eighteen and apply it to your life.

2. We have to be desperate for the very presence of God.

Yes, we need to feast on the goodness of God. We need some spiritual meat and potatoes, and we need to hunger for the Word of God.

3. We need to have a spirit of expectancy.

Another way to say it is to guard against unbelief. A move of God will not happen in our timing. It may not happen the way that we pictured it to happen. So it's time to stand on the Word of God and be willing to step out on faith.

The Lord wants to take religion by the throat and choke it out. It's not about you, it's not about me, but it is all about Jesus. Look at what Isaiah writes in Isaiah 43:18-19:

> "Forget the former things; do not dwell on the past. See, I am doing a new thing! Now it springs up; do you not perceive it? I am making a way in the desert and streams in the wasteland."

Plow the fields and prepare for rain. The Lord wants to do something new in our hearts and bring freshness back to His Church. So we must be prepared and ready to go and give His love away. It may be a lot of work, but the harvest will be worth our efforts.

> *1 Corinthians 3:5-8:* "What, after all, is Apollos? And what is Paul? Only servants, through whom you came to believe, as the Lord has assigned to each his tasks. I planted the seed, and Apollos watered it, but God made it grow. So neither he who plants nor he who waters is anything, but only God, who makes things grow. The man who plants and the man who waters have on purpose, and each will be rewarded according to his labor."

Church, the best is yet to come. Let's obey God's call and leave the results to our Heavenly Father. May God bless your talents, your efforts, and your ministries. Let our efforts bring honor and praise to the Savior of the world. To Him be the glory forever and ever. Amen.

-5-
Catch a Vision

We are at a critical time in the life of the Church. I believe Satan's time here on earth is getting short, and he is turning the heat up when it comes to persecuting the Church. Don't be surprised by what he has up his sleeves. We all know that the Devil doesn't fight fairly. He has no shame or conscience; that is a fact. He will say or do anything to tear down, cause dissension, and chaos in every believer's life.

As a Church, we all have experienced many of those God moments when God's love and grace blow us away. We can all recall those good times when we experienced growth, changed lives, and a spirit of unity. But what about those times when things are not going so well? What about when you are frustrated and tired and wonder how we got here? Maybe your Church history is like a rollercoaster. It is full of a lot of ups and downs. Are you walking through a time of testing with the Lord to see what we are made of? Is God trying to get your attention, or is it possible He wants to regain our focus to see what is important to us?

I guarantee Satan will do everything he can to discourage us. He will do whatever it takes to sidetrack us and cause a distraction. But here is the good news, if you are in Christ, you will overcome. Because of what Christ has done for us, we will move forward. We will make a difference and reach people with the Gospel of Jesus Christ.

I want to share three things that can encourage the body of believers and your ministries.

1. Ensure your vision is clear and leave no doubt about what God has called you to do.

A Church without a vision will surely die. Have you ever stopped and noticed all the dying churches all over America? So many churches started so good; years later, they could barely afford to leave the lights on. I don't have all the answers, but I believe God is always at work in this world, and there will always be things I do not understand. I read about a church that was struggling to keep its doors open. So they decide to cook some chicken and invite people from their community. It was a great success, and they raised a lot of money. Those funds keep the doors open for a few more weeks. So when that money was gone, they cooked more chicken, and the cycle continued for about two years. Eventually, the House of God became the House of Chicken. That's right; the church became a restaurant. They lost their vision. They became satisfied, complacent, and spiritually lazy. They got stuck in a spiritual rut and turned their eyes off what was most important. Their relationship with God was replaced with religion. The church became more about a tradition than following God's heart and passions.

What has God burdened your heart with? Why does your local body of believers exist? Are we reaching out to people in our community and families in our neighborhood? Are you being obedient to God's calling? What dream has God put in you? I dare you to try and answer these questions. I double-dog-dare you!

I want to challenge you, the Church, to catch a fresh vision from the living God. Know that He is alive and well and wants us to reach this lost and dying world. He is not interested in setting up a Country Club for us to enjoy. Ask

Say It Again

God for a clear vision and the guts to walk it out. Please ask the people in your local body what our purpose is. Why do we exist? Don't be scared to ask other leaders these same questions. If you all have different answers, you may all be going in different directions. More plowing gets done when we are all going in the same direction.

2. Dare to be great.

Matthew 19:26: "Jesus looked at them and said, 'With man this is impossible, but with God all things are possible."

Dare to be great. Not in self, but in the Lord. Not in our abilities, wisdom, understanding, or power. But in His abilities, knowledge, experience, and passion. With men, it is impossible, but with God, all things are possible. His power is unlimited, and we can draw from an endless power supply.

Jesus speaks these words in John 14:12: "I tell you the truth, anyone who has faith in me will do what I have been doing. He will do even greater things than these because I am going to the Father."

Can you imagine what would happen if more Christians believed that truth? How would our schools differ if we believed this truth and walked it out in faith? How would our churches change? Would we see a difference in our local, state, and federal governments? We all know all the amazing things that Jesus did when he lived here on this earth. He healed the sick and the blind. Our Lord turned water into wine. He raised the dead and spoke life into the multitudes. So, what was Jesus saying to us?

This request isn't a trick question. He told the Church that we could do those things today with faith and much more because we have the Holy Spirit. Look at what Jesus says in John 14:15-20:

> *"If you love me, you will obey what I command. And I will ask the Father, and he will give you another Counselor to be with you forever, the Spirit of truth. The world cannot accept him because it neither sees him nor knows him. But you know him, for he lives with you and will be with you. I will not leave you as orphans; I will come to you. Before long, the world will not see me anymore, but you will see me. Because I live, you also will live. On that day you will realize that I am in the Father, and you are in me, and I am in you."*

Dare to be great in the Father because the Holy Spirit lives inside everyone in Christ. Because the Holy Spirit lives in us, God can do amazing things through us if we have faith. To God be the glory! Because He lives in me, other people can be encouraged. Because He lives in me, sickness and diseases will be pushed back. Because He lives in me, the truth can be spread worldwide, and lives can be changed. "Thank you, Lord, for your promises." Don't shrink back in fear and unbelief. Don't coward away when the opposition comes, and the enemy hits you from every side. Know that you are the child of the King; He has not left us alone to fight our battles. But He has given us the gift of the Holy Spirit, which lives inside of us, to help us to stand firm and overcome. Because of the power of the Holy Spirit, we will be victorious, and we will not be defeated. So, rise up, Church, and dare to be great in the power of the Holy Spirit.

Say It Again

3. Let no one deter you from the Lord's vision.

Philippians 4:13: "I can do everything through him who gives me strength."

If you are busy with the Lord, you will have critics. If you are about the Father's business, people will talk about you and put you down. If you are consumed with Jesus, there will be persecution. For those who dream in Christ, there will be those who say, "You can't do that; we have never done it that way before." Keep in mind that our number one enemy is behind it all. It never ceases to amaze me how Satan can use 'church folks' to bring us down or discourage us from dreaming in Christ. But Satan doesn't fight fair; he will throw everything at you, even the kitchen sink. So prepare yourself for the attack of Satan himself.

I want to encourage you as a Church, don't shrink back. Listen, don't give up but continue to pursue whatever God has placed in your heart. Keep pressing forward and stay focused on your calling from God. Don't grow weary in doing good.

Isaiah 40:28-31: "Do you not know? Have you not heard? The Lord is the everlasting God, the Creator of the ends of the earth. He will not grow tired or weary, and his understanding no one can fathom. He gives strength to the weary and increases the power of the weak. Even youth grow tired and weary, and young men stumble and fall, but those who hope in the Lord will renew their strength. They will soar on wings like eagles; they will run and not grow weary, they will walk and not be faint."

Isaiah 41:10: "So do not fear, for I am with you; do not be dismayed, for I am your God. I will strengthen you and help you; I will uphold you with my righteous right hand."

What an encouraging word from Isaiah. He knew we as a Church would grow tired and weary. But he wanted to remind us of whom we serve. He is the everlasting God, the forever God of the universe. He is the One who gives us strength. He is the One who picks us up when we stumble and fall. He is the One who placed the wind in our sails. Yes, He is the God of the universe, and He loves us. He is on our side and will give us everything we need to fight. So, don't be overwhelmed, and don't be dismayed. He will uphold His Church and make sure we are strengthened and encouraged.

Charles Stanley once said, "We, the Church, are either going through life making scratches or kicking dents in the gates of hell." I don't know about you, but I want to kick some severe dents into the gates of hell. Don't allow the distractions of this world to get you sidetracked from God's call on your life. Never lose hope and sight of God's vision in your heart. God is up to something and wants to use us, the Church. What a blessing!

-6-
Refreshing

Have you ever been thirsty? Thinking about being thirsty, my mind returns to High School football. Every summer, we would have a football camp to prepare for the upcoming season. My tenth-grade year was the worst. We had three practices a day, and we had to live in the gym; this lasted for two weeks. We went home for the weekend but had to return that Sunday night to be ready for practice the next day. Those midday practices were the worst. It was ninety degrees plus with no shade, and we wore full pads and uniforms. The coaches wouldn't let us drink water except once a practice. I felt like my mouth was dry as a desert. There were times when I wondered if I was going to survive. When we finally took a break, we all ran to the water and drank as much water as possible. Talking about being refreshed, that water was like gold to us. We needed that refreshing to be able to finish practice.

> *Proverbs 11:25: "A generous man will prosper; he who refreshes others will himself be refreshed."*

What does it mean to be refreshed? What does that mean to you? To me, I think of restored strength. After reading this verse, we must stop and ask ourselves, do we refresh others? In other words, when we encounter other people, do we refresh them? Do they feel renewed or drained? Let's take it further; are we restoring our community as Christians? Do we encourage the cashier who has been standing in that one spot for eight hours? Do we refresh our kid's teachers with encouragement after a long day with thirty students? Do we tip our waiter well or give them enough to say we left a tip? Let's take another step further: Do we refresh our spouse and kids? Sometimes those close to us are the hardest to encourage because they know us the best.

As Christians, we are called to love our neighbor as ourselves. We are to consider other people's interests over our own. We are called to do everything without complaining. We are to be the light of the world and a vessel of hope and encouragement to everyone around us. That was so easy to type on my computer but much harder to live out in the real world of discouragement and strife. But it is not impossible! We are called to refresh those whom God has placed in our path. We will encounter people daily whose needs are just as real as my need for water back in High School during summer camp. They need hope, encouragement, and love.

In Romans, Paul writes about his plan to come and visit them. Look what he says in Romans 15:31-33:

> *"Pray that I may be rescued from the unbelievers in Judea and that my service in Jerusalem may be acceptable to the saints there, so that by God's will I may come to you with joy and together with you be refreshed. The God of peace is with you all. Amen."*

Paul knew the importance of being refreshed. We all get tired, down, overwhelmed, and beat up. Discouragement and depression are rampant and spreading like the Black Plague. Depression doesn't care who you are or what position you hold. If we were honest, most of us need to be refreshed. Life is hard, and the business of this life will wear you down. We, the Church, need to be a source to each other

Say It Again

and everyone around us. If we are truly going to be refreshing to the people we encounter daily, we will have to do a few things.

1. We will need to be super intentional.

We will not become carriers of hope by accident. We will not wake up one day and become a hope dealer overnight. Think like this: being a great athlete takes more than wanting to. It takes time, dedication, and much hard work. It will not happen overnight; it is a process. A great athlete has to have a drive and a passion that burns inside of them to get up every day and train. There must be a vision of where they want to go and what they want to be. Great athletes are willing to push themselves past their comfort zone and become uncomfortable to get better. They are super intentional when it comes to their training.

Are we, as believers, super intentional regarding being refreshed or refreshing others? What can we do? What do we need to change in our lives? Just like a great athlete, it will take time and discipline. Just because God placed this on your heart today doesn't mean you will wake up tomorrow ready to refresh the world. Begin to ask God to up your awareness of people around you that need a word of encouragement. Ask the Lord to give you a drive, passion for His Word, and hunger to know Him more intimately. Have a plan and set goals to get to where God asks you to go. When those plans are in place, and those goals are set, find someone to hold you accountable. Don't be scared to place reminders and sticky notes of what God is showing and calling you to. Set aside time each day to be refreshed by the Lord. It has to be your greatest priority. Some may call it discipline, but I call it my greatest joy. To be a hope dealer, we must first receive from God's goodness. The more you receive, the more you can give away.

2. We have to reprogram our default mode.

Romans 12:1-2: "Therefore, I urge you, brothers, in the view of God's mercy, to offer your bodies as living sacrifices, holy and pleasing to God; this is your spiritual act of worship. Do not conform to the pattern of this world, but be transformed by the renewing of your mind. Then you will be able to test and approve what God's will is his good, pleasing, and perfect will."

What a powerful, life-changing scripture. Paul is urging the Church to set aside selfishness and pride. He encourages us to offer our bodies as a living sacrifice and dares us to be different. He challenges us not to be just like everyone else or do whatever it takes to fit in. But we are called to be different. We are called to follow Jesus's way of living. We are called to reprogram how we think and carry ourselves when things don't go our way. In other words, how do you respond when you don't get a fair shake? Do we want to lash out and lose our temper? Do we show out and let them know what we think of them? What about that person who is going under the speed limit and you are already late for church? Do you get mad, frustrated, and sometimes angry? Then you let them know what you think about their driving as you speed around them. Hopefully, they will not pull behind you into the church's parking lot.

Who do we lose it with the most? They are usually the ones we love the most. It's our family or those closest to us. We must reprogram our default mode to be the Church God calls us to be. Do we reflect our Lord Jesus Christ when difficult times come? Do we show mercy and grace to others

Say It Again

when difficult people enter our space? Do we control our temper and constantly renew our minds? God's Word tells us that the old has gone, and the new has come. In Christ, we are a new creation. He has come to take over, and He has come to rule and reign upon the throne of our hearts.

> *James 1:19-21: "My dear brothers, take note of this: Everyone should be quick to listen, slow to speak and slow to become angry, for man's anger does not bring about the righteous life that God desires. Therefore, get rid of all moral filth and the evil that is so prevalent and humbly accept the word planted in you, which can save you."*

We must fill our minds and heart with God's Word to reprogram our default mode. Selfishness and pride have to go. There needs to be a time of confession and repentance at the feet of Jesus. Yes, a time when we lay everything on the altar and ask the Lord to forgive us sins and shortcomings, and screw-ups. Then ask the Father to fill you with His goodness, compassion, and grace. The more I have of Him, the less I will respond in selfishness and pride. The more I have of Him, the less I think of myself and more about others. There needs to be more of Him and less of me until it is all of Him and none of me. The more I have of Him, the less I want to impress others. The more I have of Him, the less I desire the spotlight. The more I have of Him, the less I apologize for my words in anger.

To be refreshed, we need to reprogram the default mode of our hearts. We must be more careful about what we take in through our eyes and ears. We must guard what we feed our minds and ensure we are feasting on God's Holy Word. Take every thought captive and be intentional about what you feed your soul. Put into action what God is sharing with you daily. Walk it out!

> *James 1:22-25: "Do not merely listen to the word, and so deceive yourselves. Do what it says. Anyone who listens to the word but does not do what it says is like a man who looks at his face in a mirror and, after looking at himself, goes away and immediately forgets what he looks like. But the man who looks intently into the perfect law that gives freedom, and continues to do this, not forgetting what he has heard, but doing it, he will be blessed in what he does."*

3. Be refreshed by the ultimate source: Jesus Christ.

How many carry emotional, spiritual, and mental burdens beyond our abilities? You know, those things that weigh us down and leave us empty and tired. That emptiness and fatigue will affect our emotions, relationships, and decisions. Are you sick and tired of being tired?

> *Matthew 11:28-30: "Come to me, all you who are weary and burdened, and I will give you rest. Take my yoke upon you and learn from me, for I am gentle and humble in heart, and you will find rest for your souls. For my yoke is easy and my burden is light."*

In other words, God wants to carry the weight too heavy for us to move, and He does that through a personal relationship with Jesus. As a result, we can find ourselves worn out, hurting, and limited. Not because God is asking too much of us but because we insist on carrying too much. Instead of letting Jesus take our weight in His strength, our pride pushes us to preach better, love harder, and reach more people. The Lord knows all about our pride and oversized egos. He knows everything about us.

> *Psalm 103:13-14: "As a father has compassion on his children, so the Lord has compassion on those who fear him; for he knows how we are formed, he remembers that we were dust."*

Take time today and ask yourself, what unnecessary weight am I carrying today? Is it the burden of having to be perfect? It may be yesterday's blunders or your past. It may be your past performance or even a sin that haunts you. We all have something that hinders us in our walk with Christ. But know this, your failure or past sins do not frame your future. Our Heavenly Father cares for us. He loves us unconditionally. Our Lord wants to refresh you and restore your joy and passion for life. He wants to regain your strength and fill you with a heart of praise. Look at what Jesus said to the woman at the well in John 4:13-14:

> *"Everyone who drinks this water will be thirsty again, but whoever drinks the water I give him will never thirst. Indeed, the water I give him will become in him a spring of water welling up to eternal life."*

Jesus is offering us a source of refreshment. He desires to refresh us and fill us with all His goodness. He will give us the wisdom and strength to raise our kids and keep our marriages pure and holy. There is hope in the name of Jesus. There is power in the life-giving blood of Jesus Christ. So run into His presence and soak in the love of God. It will transform you and refresh you.

Don't put on that mask and pretend that everything is ok. God wants to break down the wall of pride and selfishness. He wants us to break away from the standard and experience life change today.

-7-
A New Thing

Family, what can I say? I can sit here and type all day long about all the great memories and great times I have spent with my family. I could type out multiple stories of things that happened in the past that would make you laugh and roll on the floor. I could tell you about family vacations and family get-togethers that are still fresh in my mind. It all happened years ago, but it seems like yesterday. Where would we be without family? But, when it comes to family, there is a lot of give and take. Yes, family is great, but issues will always pop up. There will always be those family discussions you can't avoid or escape. How about those awkward moments when someone says what is on their mind, and no one knows what to say or how to respond? Don't you love your family? Sometimes we have to take the good with the bad.

Think about it this way; our Church is also considered our family—the family of God. As with our physical family, there is much giving and taking when it comes to our Church family. Over the year, I want you to think about all the good times you had with your Church family. If you are like me, you could think about hundreds of occasions when you grew up in the Lord, laughed with others, enjoyed great meals, and praised the Living God together. What about all those difficult times that popped up over the years? Sometimes, you didn't quite agree with all the decisions or the misunderstandings that caused strife among friends. When difficult times come, there is always one constant thing, God is faithful. The Word of God tells us that He will never leave or forsake us.

During those difficult times, we, the Church, are tempted to doubt God. We will tend to murmur and complain. There will be anxiety and stress that will grow and will cause us to fall to sin. During those times, we, the Church, tend to lose focus and passion for the things that matter. Somehow, we forget how faithful God has been to us, just like the children of Israel. Take a look at Psalm 78:40-43; 52-56:

> *"How often they rebelled against him in the desert and grieved him in the wasteland! Again and again, they put God to the test; they vexed the Holy One of Israel. They did not remember his power-the day he redeemed them from the oppressor, the day he displayed his miraculous signs in Egypt, his wonders in the region of Zoan. But he brought his people out like a flock; he led them like sheep through the desert. He guided them safely, so they were unafraid, but the sea engulfed their enemies. Thus he brought them to the border of his holy land, to the hill country his right hand had taken. He drove out nations before them and allotted their land to them as an inheritance; he settled the tribes of Israel in their homes. But they put God to the test and reeled against the Most High; they did not keep his statutes."*

The Lord looked over Israel and protected them from the evil hand of Pharaoh. He cared for their every need and placed a shelter of protection around them, yet they didn't remain faithful to His statutes. How many times has God blessed us, and we take that for granted? We question His love and faithfulness. Sometimes we doubt God and His ability to care for us, our family, and our Church. We seem to have the same tendency that Israel did when they were released from bondage in Egypt. How often do we allow difficult circumstances to overwhelm or cloud our view? How often do we run off in fear and forget the faithfulness of our Heavenly Father?

> *Isaiah 40:28-31: "Do you not know? Have you not heard? The Lord is the everlasting God, the Creator of the ends of the earth. He will not grow tired or weary, and his understanding no one can fathom. He gives strength to the weary and increases the power of the weak. Even youths grow tired and weary, and young men stumble and fall, but those who hope in the Lord will renew their strength. They will soar on wings like eagles; they will run and not grow weary, they will walk and not be faint."*

What an encouragement to the Church today. You see, we serve a God that is everlasting and faithful. He is the God of yesterday, today, and forever. He doesn't get tired and weary, but He gives wisdom and strength to those who are worn down and discouraged. He extends His hand of mercy to those who are frustrated and defeated. He is a God that brings hope and encouragement to those who have given up. He breathes life into our lungs and fills us with passion. He is able. Yes, He is able. What an awesome God we serve! Take a look at what Isaiah says in Isaiah 41:10:

> *"So do not fear, for I am with you; do not be dismayed, for I am your God. I will strengthen you and help you; I will uphold you with my righteous right hand."*

What a promise for those whose hope is in the Lord Jesus Christ. What a mighty God we serve. Why should we fear? Why should we be dismayed or coward away when things get tough? We have the promise from His Holy Word that He will be there for us and uphold us with His righteous hands. When we face that God-sized challenge, He will help us through those stormy waters. He is the great Redeemer and the lover of my soul. Isaiah tells us this in Isaiah 43:2-3:

> *"When you pass through the waters, I will be with you; and when you pass through the rivers, they will not sweep over you. When you walk through the fire, the flames will not set you ablaze. For I am the Lord, your God, the Holy One of Israel, your Savior."*

In Christ, we are overcomers. In Christ, we will not be defeated. In Christ, we will make a difference. In Christ, the Church will stand the test of time. The Church of Jesus Christ will make a difference in this world. Never forget that our God is able, and He is faithful. Listen, God wants to use you to reach this lost and dying world, and He is right there by our sides to equip us and encourage us. Look at what Paul tells us in Ephesians 3:20:

> *"Now to him who is able to do immeasurable more than all we ask or imagine, according to his power that is at work within us, to him be glory in the church and in Christ Jesus throughout all generations, forever and ever! Amen."*

I pray you can receive this message that Paul is handing to the Church of Christ today. We are limited in talent, wisdom, strength, and endurance. We may not have the best abilities, the greatest education, or a great singing voice. But if you are in Christ, the Holy Spirit lives in you, and the hope of all glory dwells inside you. He will give us everything we need to complete the mission that God has called us to in Matthew chapter twenty-eight. He will take our willingness and our limited resources and multiply them to achieve His work. What an awesome God! He wants to use us to change the world. He wants to do the miraculous through a willing vessel. Are you ready to be blown away by the power of God?

> *Isaiah 43:18-19: "Forgetting the former things; do not dwell on the past. See, I am doing a new thing! Now it springs up; do you not perceive it? I am making a way in the desert and streams in the wasteland."*

The Lord has been faithful to His Church, and we have seen some incredible works of God. He had seen us through difficult times and strengthened us when we thought we couldn't keep going. But we haven't seen anything yet. His best work is still in front of us. God calls His Church a lighthouse in this lost and dying world. We are called to reach out to our family and friends and let them know that the Creator of heaven and earth loves them. We are called to fight for our children and our students. We are called to share the Good News of Jesus Christ. We have to tell the world about the cross of Christ, borrowed tomb, and our risen Savior. This world needs to know that there is hope and that hope is found in Jesus! The Savior of the world. In Jesus, you can experience grace, mercy, and eternal joy. Because of our calling, God is asking His Church to do four things. To share this new thing, we must make ourselves available in four ways.

1. We must repent.

When did you last fall on your face before a Holy God? When did you last have a heart-to-heart conversation with your Heavenly Father? When was the last time you pushed pretense to the side, dropped your religious guard, and had an honest conversation with your Maker? He is calling his Church to repentance. Looking at David's conversation with the Lord when he was overwhelmed by his sin with Bathsheba in Psalm 51:1-12:

> *"Have mercy on me, O God, according to your unfailing love; according to your great compassion blot out my transgressions. Wash away all my iniquity and cleanse me from my sin. For I know my transgressions, and my sin is always before me. Against you, you only, have I sinned and done what is evil in your sight, so that you are proved right when you speak and justified when you judge. Surely I was sinful at birth, sinful from the time my mother conceived me. Surely you desire truth in the inner parts, you teach me wisdom in the inmost place. Cleanse me with hyssop, and I will be clean; wash me and I will be whiter than snow. Let me hear joy and gladness; let the bones you have crushed rejoice. Hide your face from my sins and blot out all my iniquities. Create in me, a pure heart, O God, and renew a steadfast spirit within me. Do not cast me from your presence or take your Holy Spirit from me. Restore to me the joy of your salvation and grant me a willing spirit, to sustain me."*

David gives us an excellent go-by prayer when sin enters our lives. Can you sense David's raw emotions after he is caught in that adulterous relationship with Bathsheba? David pushed aside all pretense, dropped his religious guard, and openly confessed his sin to the Lord. He came clean and admitted his guilt and shame. Then he asked the Lord to forgive him and to cleanse his sinful heart, then begged God to restore the joy of his salvation. The Lord heard David's prayer and restored him. He washed his evil nature and showed him grace. What an awesome God we serve.

Is there a sin you need to confess? Is there something in your past that haunts you to this day? Are regrets lingering in the soul holding you back and stopping you from going deeper in your relationship with the Lord? It is time to give it all to your Heavenly Father and lay it at his feet. Hold nothing back, and pour your heart out in a time of confession. Ask Him to forgive and cleanse you from all your sins and regrets. Ask Him to restore your joy and fill you with His goodness. Rid yourself of anything that is not of God and put on love, compassion, integrity, and all the things of God. It is time to be renewed and refreshed. It is time to repent, Church.

2. We need to make it all about Jesus.

First Corinthians 2:1-5: "When I came to you, brothers, I did not come with eloquence or superior wisdom as I proclaimed to you the testimony about God. For I resolved to know nothing while I was with you except Jesus Christ and him crucified. I came to you in weakness and fear and with much trembling. My message and my preaching were not with wise and persuasive words, but with a demonstration of the Spirit's power so that your faith might not rest on men's wisdom, but on God's power."

We are not enough. In other words, our wisdom, gifts, and abilities are insufficient to accomplish what God has called us to do. We need Jesus to come in and take over; selfishness and pride must go. It is time to kick 'self' off the throne of our hearts and seat Him in the driver's seat of our soul. We, the Church, must make it all about Jesus and take our hands off His glory.

As His Church, why do we do what we do? Who are we giving the glory to? Who do we place on the pedestal to adore? We all know the correct answer, but it is so easy to fall into the trap of pride. Sometimes, we put a ton of work into the Church and the mission of Christ, and it is good to get a pat on the back or a hand clap. But it doesn't take much to get us sideways, and before you know it, we run off the road in a spiritual ditch. We must remind ourselves along our journey that it's not about us. It should be all about Him — more of Him and less of me.

3. We have to make prayer a priority in our lives.

Whether we know it or not, a spiritual war rages around us. Satan's time is running short, and he is amping up the pressure a notch or two. Take time to pause and look around you; families are falling apart. Spirits of depression, anxiety, worry, and stress surround us. Selfishness and pride are at an all-time high, and we can't take our eyes off ourselves. Yet, we know this war isn't fought by flesh and blood but in the spirit. Look what Paul says in Ephesians 6:12:

> *For our struggle is not against flesh and blood, but against the rulers, against authorities, against the powers of this dark world, and against the spiritual forces of evil in the heavenly realms."*

Say It Again

Church, it is time to fight! We have wasted enough time doing things with our strength and wisdom. We need to drop on our knees and pray to the God above and ask Him to pour out His Spirit and move like never before in the life of His Church. Let's get honest with each other. I want to ask you three questions. The first question: How much time do you spend on your phone daily? Second question: How much time do you spend in prayer, talking with your Heavenly Father daily? Third question: Which is more significant? Why do most churches not reach people and share God's love?

If you ever study Church history, you will see one thing repeatedly. Before any move of God, God's people made praying a priority. Take a look at the early Church in Acts 1:14:

"They all joined together constantly in prayer, along with the women and Mary the mother of Jesus, and with his brothers."

Acts 2:42-43: "They devoted themselves to the apostles teaching and to the fellowship, to the breaking of bread and to prayer. Everyone was filled with awe, and many wonders and miraculous signs were done by the apostles."

The early Church loved getting together and fellowshipping with each other, but they were also people of prayer. They were willing to meet together and poured their hearts into the Lord. The Word tells us that they met daily in the temple to worship, praise the Lord, and pray. Then great things happened all around them. Many miracles and wonders were happening every day.

> *Second Chronicles 7:14: "If my people, who are called by name, will humble themselves and pray and seek my face and turn from their wicked ways, then will I hear from heaven and will for their sin and will heal their land."*

When we become a family of prayer, God will begin to do a 'new thing' in our hearts and the community around us.

> *Ephesians 3:20: "Now to him who is able to do immeasurably more than all we ask or imagine, according to his power that is at work within us."*

Last, we must push the Word of God to the forefront of everything we do. We, the Church, need to dive deep into the Holy Scriptures.

> *Hebrews 4:12: "For the word of God is living and active. Sharper than any double-edged sword, it penetrates even to diving soul and spirit, joints and marrow; it judges the thoughts and attitudes of the heart."*

I guarantee we have a couple of Bibles set around our homes. It usually sits in the same place and never gets picked up. The Word of God needs to be our constant companion. We need to hide it in our hearts, memorize it, and meditate on its every word. Church; we need to become students and God's Word and stand on the truths and not be shaken. The Bible is God's love letter to His children. Let it go deep into your soul and feast on the buffet of eternal truths of God.

Say It Again

God is doing a new thing! It is not about a new program or adding a new ministry. It is about the Church of the Living God repenting their sins and dying to themselves. It's about the Church making it all about Jesus and falling on our faces before God in prayer. Then we must dive deep into God's Holy Word and allow it to consume our thoughts and actions. Finally, we have to get ready for a great move of God.

-8-
Stay Focused

The Christian life is a journey. We see so many things and face so many difficult situations. We must make tough decisions every day. Yes, there are those mountain-top experiences, but we all hit nearby valleys too. We all seem to stay so busy. Think about all those times you were running kids to ball practice, meeting deadlines at work, and rushing to make it to all the church activities. Don't forget all the family stuff with the homework, school projects, and unexpected things that pop up. Boy, do we live a busy life? So many times, we complain about being so busy, yet we always seem to need something going on.

In business, we find ourselves drifting away from God. Still going to church and being involved because we must check off the boxes. Somehow, we got off track and took our eyes off Jesus. Then we find ourselves focused on the things of this world. What happened? Where did we go wrong? How did I end up so spiritually dry and empty?

I love March Madness. No, it's not a shopping sale at the Mall, but it is the end-of-the-season College Basketball Tournament. Some of the country's top college basketball teams are invited to compete for the title of National Champion. Sixty-four teams come and play, and only the strong survive and move on to the next round. Then when it is all said and done, it comes down to the final two teams. Every year there seem to be some upsets. Things happen in each game that keeps you on the edge of your seat. There is plenty of drama, tension, and a huge storyline. But it all comes down to the final two teams and those last few free

Say It Again

throws to see who wins the games—talking about the pressure that falls on that one player. The game came down to this one shot in the final seconds. You hit this free throw and win your team's National Championship. You will be a hero. If you miss it, your team will lose the game. Talking about pressure, you are in a pressure cooker.

As they are about to shoot this last shot, the arena is packed, people are watching all over the nation on TV, and everyone in the stands is screaming and waving to distract the player from making this critical shot. Do you get the picture? The player must focus, see the rim, make a smooth shot, and watch it go in. But all around him is chaos and distractions. So the key for him to make this shot is to shut everything out and see that rim.

Doesn't that sound just like the life of a Christian? We are called to follow the life of Jesus and run after Him with everything we have. But Satan is doing everything he can to cause distractions and chaos around us. Satan knows if he can get us to take our eyes off the goal of knowing our Heavenly Father. He can make us miss our shot. The thief comes to kill, steal, and destroy. Satan also comes to distract us, the Church, from our gaze on Jesus.

What can we do to stay focused? What can we do to help us not fall into all the distractions Satan throws at us? How can we remain focused on the most important things and the things that bring glory to God? I want to give you three simple encouragements that will help us in our gaze on Jesus and keep us getting side-tracked with the worries of this world.

1. Keep your eyes on Christ.

Matthew 14:22-27: "Immediately Jesus made the disciples get into the boat and go on ahead of him to the other side, while he dismissed the crowd. After he dismissed them, he went up on a mountainside by himself to pray. When evening came, he was there alone, but the boat was already a considerable distance from land, buffeted by waves because the wind was against it. During the fourth watch of the night, Jesus went out to them, walking on the lake. When the disciples saw him walking on the lake, they were terrified. 'It's a ghost.' they said and cried out in fear. But Jesus immediately said to them: 'Take courage! It is I. Don't be afraid.'"

Jesus just fed the 5000 with five loaves and two fish. What an amazing miracle of God. All of Jesus' disciples were there, and they saw this amazing work from the hands of Jesus. Everyone ate and was satisfied. The people enjoyed this incredible buffet, ate until their bellies were full, and had twelve baskets of leftovers! Can you imagine being there that day? Seeing Jesus face to face, watching a miracle of God happening right before your eyes, enjoying a great meal, and experiencing something you will never forget.

But place yourself in the disciple's shoes. Yes, they experienced this same miracle, which changed their lives forever, but they didn't get to kick back and enjoy the feast. Instead, they had to serve the people. There was no time to eat, take your sandals off, and share jokes with friends. They had to help all these men and their families. Can you imagine what they had to put up with that day? How long did it take to serve this many people? I know one thing had to be accurate, they were dog-tired. That means they were physically wore-out. All they wanted to do was clean up and head home. Yet, Jesus sent them to paddle across a lake. I am sure no one complained, right?

Say It Again

While they were paddling across the lake, a storm blew in. They began to think, what else can happen? Can it get any worse? Then they saw an image walking toward them on the water. Yes, it could get worse! They thought it was a ghost. Then they all began to cry out in fear. At that point, Jesus revealed his identity and told them not to be afraid. The disciples had to be thinking this was a long, difficult day. Have you ever had days like that? Take a look at what happens next in Matthew 14:28-33:

> *"Lord, if it's you," Peter replied, 'tell me to come to you on the water.' 'Come,' he said. Then Peter got down out of the boat, walked on water, and came toward Jesus. But when he saw the wind, he was afraid and, beginning to sink, cried out, 'Lord save me!' Immediately Jesus reached out his hand and caught him. 'You of little faith,' he said, 'why did you doubt?' Then he climbed into the boat, the wind died down. Then those who were in the boat worshiped him, saying, 'Truly you are the Son of God.'"*

If anyone would get out of the boat in a storm and walk to Jesus, it would be Peter. He was always the one who had an opinion and was ready to express himself freely. I am sure all the other disciples there that day were thinking, here he goes again. He always has to be at the center of attention. That may be true, but Peter was the only one who ever walked on water besides Jesus.

Can you see Peter that night? Can you imagine what was going through his mind when he requested to come to Jesus on the water in a storm? Then Jesus told him to come to Him. Peter was full of faith. Peter's eyes were locked in on Jesus' face when he took that first step on that water. As Peter walked to Jesus, his eyes wandered from Jesus' face, and he began to see the waves. The fear flooded his heart, and he began to sink. Peter cried to Jesus when he started to sink, "Lord, save me!" Jesus reached out and grabbed Peter by the hand and pulled him out of the waves. As they returned to the boat, the waters became calm.

You may be in that place where Peter was so long ago. You are tired; you have been faithfully serving others for some time. You started so well but have taken your eyes off Christ over time. You are sinking under the world's pressure, and your time alone with God is nonexistent. Your prayers seem powerless and never seem to rise above the ceilings. You are struggling to keep your head above the water.

I encourage you to keep your eyes centered on Christ. Don't let your eyes wander from His presence. Make sure that your time alone with Him is the most important thing you do daily. To stay focused as a body of believers, we must keep our eyes on the most important thing. That is our personal relationship with Jesus Christ. Yes, storms will brew up, and things will happen while serving others. But don't let those things distract us from our gaze on Jesus.

2. Return to your first love.

Jesus said in Revelation 2:4-5: "Yet I hold this against you: You have forsaken your first love. Remember the height from which you have fallen! Repent and do the things you did at first. If you do not repent, I will come to you and remove your lampstand from its place."

Revelation 2:4-5 is a strong word from Jesus to the Church of Ephesus. He didn't hesitate to tell them that they had forsaken their first love and had left the former devotion they once had for Him. I am sure these words didn't fall on

Say It Again

deaf ears. I am pretty sure Jesus got their attention that day. What about you? Can you remember when you accepted Jesus as the Lord and Savior of your life? Do you remember the excitement and the joy you experienced when He forgave you of your sin and filled us with His amazing love? You couldn't wait to tell everybody about what Christ has done for you. Your time alone with God was amazing; you learned so much daily. His presence was so strong, and He spoke so clearly to your listening ears. Those were the days.

Have you ever approached someone you have not seen in years and told them, "You have not changed a bit?" That is probably not a true statement. People constantly change, but we change so slowly that it is hard to notice them. The same is true with relationships. Relationships are constantly evolving. They are either growing or dying. To say that a relationship is sitting still is a lie. What has happened to your first love? I am talking about your relationship with Jesus Christ. Have you been pulled away from the Lord by the subtle waves of business? Are you wondering how did I fall away from the One who gave Himself for me on that cross? It changed so slowly that you didn't even notice how far you had left your relationship with Jesus.

Return to your first love. Return to that former devotion that you once had with Christ. How? Repent.

> *1 John 1:9: "If we confess our sins, he is faithful and just and will forgive us our sins and purify us from all unrighteousness."*

What a promise we have from the Lord Jesus. We, as His children, can come boldly to His throne of grace and pour out our hearts to Him. Is there a sin we need to confess? Is there something we need to get right with the

God of the universe? Have we strayed from the very presence of God and started doing our own thing? The time is now; stop putting it off, and confess your sins and shortcoming to a God that loves you more than anything. Get back to reading His Word and talking and listening to His voice. Seek His direction and wisdom for daily living, and let the peace of God rule in your heart.

3. Hold firm to your faith.

Hebrews 4:14-16: "Therefore, since we have a great high priest who has gone through the heavens, Jesus the Son of God, let us hold firmly to the faith we profess. For we do not have a high priest who is unable to sympathize with our weaknesses, but we have one who has been tempted in every way, just as we are- yet was without sin. Let us then approach the throne of grace with confidence, so that we may receive mercy and find grace to help us in our time of need."

God didn't leave us to fend for ourselves. Christ in me, the hope of all glory, lives inside us. The Father sent us the Holy Spirit to come alongside us to lead, guide, and direct us in His ways. Jesus knows exactly what we are going through and what we face each day. He has been tempted in every way. He met those same distractions. I encourage you to open your heart to the One who knows exactly what you are facing. Pour your heart out to Him, and share your concerns and heartaches. He truly cares for you. Don't be afraid to ask for help to face the worries of this life. Don't hesitate to ask for wisdom to deal with the schemes of the devil and the distractions of life. Hold firm to your faith. Don't let go.

Say It Again

Hebrews 3:12-13: "See to it, brothers, that none of you has a sinful, unbelieving heart that turns away from the living God. But encourage one another daily, as long as it is called Today, so that none of you may be hardened by sin's deceitfulness."

To hold firm to our faith, not only do we need the Holy Spirit, but we also need to lean on solid Christian friends around us. Make sure to surround yourself with godly friends who keep you on point and give you encouragement and sound advice. Let's all press into Christ and be that voice of encouragement to everyone we meet.

God wants to do amazing work in us and through His Church. But we, as the Church, must stay focused on the prize of knowing Christ. When distractions come along and Satan raises his ugly head, we need to get back to the basics of our Christian faith. We need to keep our eyes on Jesus and keep sight of what is most important. We need to return to our first love. Repent any sin or regret haunting our spirit and turn it over to the Lord. Then we must hold firm to our faith and surround ourselves with godly friends who will hold us accountable and support us with love and wisdom. Stay focused on Jesus!

-9-
From Existing to Really Living

How many Christians today are stuck in a dull routine of doing church? I know that is a difficult question to start this chapter, but there is no sense in beating around the bush. I don't want to be negative, but I want to confront an issue God has laid on my heart. Where is the passion for God's Word and for the things of God? What has happened to our 'want to' when loving others to Christ? What is our want to? It's an intense desire to want more. Are you tired of living the mundane Christian life?

Satan is doing his best to rock the Church to sleep while trying to destroy you and your family. He is a thief and wants to take everything you hold close to your heart. He wants to rob you of the joy of your salvation. Are you tired of repeatedly checking boxes and walking through the same routine of church life? How many of us just exist, and it seems like we are in a rut, and there is no way of getting out?

There comes a time when we must stand up and say, "Enough is enough!" Now is the time to plant your feet and declare that you are sick and tired of being sick and tired. Are you ready to move from existing to really living? If so, open your heart to what the Holy Spirit wants to show you, and get ready to receive a word from the Lord.

> *First Corinthians 1:9: "God, who called you into fellowship with the Son Jesus Christ our Lord, is faithful."*

Say It Again

The Creator of the entire universe desires a love relationship with us. Can you receive this truth today? In other words, He wants to fellowship with you and me. Likewise, the Father desires to communicate with us. Communication involves two things, talking and listening. Not only does He want us to call out to Him and express our needs and wants, but He wants us to stop long enough to listen to what He is saying back to us. When it comes to our communication with the Lord, how much time do we spend talking with the Lord? How much time do we spend listening to our Heavenly Father? Take a look at what Jesus says in Matthew 16:12-15:

> *"I have much more to say to you, more than you can now bear. But when he, the Spirit of truth, comes, he will guide you into all truth. He will not speak on his own; he will speak only what he hears, and he will tell you what is yet to come. He will bring glory to me by taking from what is mine and making it known to you. All that belongs to the Father is mine. That is why I said the Spirit will take from what is mine and make it known to you."*

The Lord always speaks and desires to share His most intimate truth with those who love Him. So here is my question: are we listening? Are we slowing down enough to hear the voice of God? Our responsibility as a child of God is to listen and obey. That's right; we must hear God's voice and fully follow His shares. But, unfortunately, sometimes we have difficulty hearing the Lord's voice and try our best to make it so complicated.

A pastor mentored me, and his name was Peter Lord. He wrote a book called "Hearing God." If you have never read this book, you must get it soon. It is a must-read to understand how to hear the Lord. In his book, he shares with his readers two things that are needed if you want to listen to the voice of God.

1. We have to have a listening ear.

In other words, we must set aside time away from all of the distractions of life to hear from the Lord. In today's world, that is easier said than done. We need to turn off all the noise that surrounds us. The world tends to shout, and the shouting never ceases. But God prefers to whisper His instructions. Set that phone off to the side, or better yet, turn it off and place it in another room. That is so hard for us to do because we think we may miss a call, an important email, or that like from our latest post.

The last thing the devil wants us to do as believers is to turn our focus to the Lord. So, don't be surprised when distractions come your way. We have to be more intentional when it comes to hearing the voice of God. Set aside time each day to get away, still our hearts and mind, and turn our attention to our Heavenly Father. Ask Him to speak and then ask for understanding. Finally, go to that quiet place where you can escape all the noise and enter His presence with worship.

2. We need a pure heart.

As believers in Jesus Christ, our hearts should be free from contamination and sin. We must confess our sins and ask for forgiveness for our shortcomings. That is an elementary part of our faith. But there is a second piece of having a pure heart that I want to present to you today. It's having the desire and commitment to one thing and purpose. Let me illustrate what I am talking about. Pure gold is a valuable commodity and is highly desired. Not only is pure gold free of rocks, dirt, or coal, but it is also free of other valuable things such as silver, diamonds, and jewels. It is 100 percent pure gold which makes it more valuable.

David was a man after God's own heart. Why? Because he stopped and took time to hear the voice of God. He took time to listen to what God was saying. Did he always obey His voice and follow God's instruction to a tee? Not always. But when David messed up and fell short of what God called him to do, he confessed his sins before the Lord. Look at Psalm 51:7-10:

> *"Cleanse me with hyssop, and I will be clean; wash me, and I will be whiter than snow. Let me hear joy and gladness; let the bones you have crushed rejoice. Hide your face from my sins and blot out all my iniquity. Create in me a pure heart, O God, and renew a steadfast spirit within me."*

David took time to hear God's voice and to ask God to cleanse his heart, but he also asked God for a desire and commitment to one thing and one purpose. Look at what David prayed for in Psalm 27:4:

> *"One thing I ask of the Lord, this is what I seek: that I may dwell in the house of the Lord all the days of my life, to gaze upon the beauty of the Lord and to seek him in his temple."*

David desired to seek, gaze, and dwell with the Lord. In other words, David wanted to seek the Lord, to sit at the feet of Jesus and soak in His presence. He wanted to gaze at

Jesus and glance at everything else. David wanted to live in a constant relationship with the Lord, abiding by a godly lifestyle. David knew what it took to hear the voice of God.

I want to share a truth that you need to hang on to and not let go of. I hope you are ready for it. Here we go. The greater the purity, the greater the power. Since this is true, how do we get a deep spiritual cleansing? How do we walk this out in our life so we are walking in purity? I am so glad you asked. I want to share an easy ten-step process you can walk through when you need a deep spiritual cleansing.

Think about it this way; there is nothing as messy and aggravating as a clogged drain, especially the sinks in the bathroom. Over time different things fall into the sink and find their way down the drain. The collection of objects builds up, clogs the drain, and stops the water flow. Because of the buildup, the water begins to back up in the sink. Then you jump into action and grab the Drano, clothes hanger, or whatever you think will free the blockage. All we want is for the water to flow through the drain again.

Here is my question, how is the flow of the Spirit in your life? Is there sin clogging up the spiritual drain and not allowing the flow of God to move in your life? The greatest hindrance to the flow of God isn't a problem of motivation but one of accumulation. Christians often experience frustration and defeat in their spiritual lives due to a nasty buildup of unconfessed sin.

> 1 John 1:9: "If we confess our sins, He is faithful and just to forgive our sins and to cleanse us from all unrighteousness."

Unconfessed sin blocks God's flow and movement in our lives, but confession is the tool we need to free up our spiritual drain and end our frustration and aggravation. We

Say It Again

need an excellent spiritual cleaning and experience freedom and joy again in our relationship with Jesus. I encourage you to follow this simple ten-step spiritual cleansing process and not rush through it.

1. **Find a quiet place to sit alone for at least one hour with a sheet of paper, something to write with, and your Bible.**

2. **Quiet your heart before the Lord by sitting still. Leave your phone in another room and push aside all distractions.**

3. **Begin to pray to the Lord and thank Him for bringing you to this place. Let the Lord know you are committed to getting your heart right with Him and unclogging your spiritual drain.**

4. **Ask Him to reveal your sins one by one.**

5. **Begin to list everything the Holy Spirit reveals to you. Don't ignore the difficult ones.**

6. **Confess your sins one at a time to the Lord. Go through your list no matter how many sins you have listed. Tell Him how sorry you are, and ask Him to forgive and cleanse you.**

7. **Anticipate the personal struggle you will face. Fight the desire to run away and forget this whole process.**

8. **Make restoration wherever necessary and expect to humble yourself to at least one person.**

9. **Write done on your paper. Receive His forgiveness and grace. Yes, say it out loud to your Heavenly Father.**

10. **Thank the Lord for forgiving and showing you so much grace. Thank Him for cleansing your spiritual drain and allowing the flow of the Spirit to move in your life once again. Praise Him for His endless love, and enjoy His fellowship.**

Not only do we need a deep spiritual cleansing, but we need a circumcised heart. A circumcised heart has had everything that is not of God cut away. Even the good things hinder God's best. Heart circumcision takes care of the good but unnecessary things that crowd God out. What is crowding God out in your life? This heart surgery will place God in the position of the highest priority.

Let me try and wrap this up. I know this is a lot to take in one chapter, but I pray that you don't rush through but take the time to get things right with the Lord. I want to encourage you to take the time you need to hear the voice of God. Get away from the distractions of this world. Ask God for a pure heart and tell Him you will work with Him through these ten steps. Tell Him you love the praise of man too much and ask Him to deliver you from that. Then ask Him to tell you the first step He wants you to take, cutting away the unnecessary good things hindering His best. Then listen to His voice and obey all the little details He shares with you.

Do you want to move from existing to really living? What are you waiting on? Seek, gaze, and dwell. Ask the Lord to give you a listening ear and a pure heart. Confess

Say It Again

your sins and ask God to remove all the unnecessary things blocking God's best. The greater the purity, the greater the power. Let's go!

-10-
Take Another Look

Our perspective is the way we interpret what's happening around us. It can either make us or break us. Our perspective shapes us; it determines how we think and react to others. Perspective creates opportunities to grow, or it hinders us as we walk through life. If our perspective leans towards the negative, we may be unaware of it. Thinking the worst can become second nature because we have been like this for so long.

> *Colossians 3:1-2: "Since, then, you have been raised with Christ, set your hearts on things above, where Christ is seated at the right hand of God. Set your minds on things above, not on earthly things."*

The negative perspective says I can't, I could never, and that is impossible. Not only that, but we tend to see the bad in other people and every situation. An optimistic perspective says I can, I will, and it will be OK. They choose to see the good in people and every situation. The faith-filled perspective says, "I can do all things through Christ that strengthens me, and I am more than a conqueror." They also believe that with God, all things are possible. A faith-filled perspective says failure is a part of growth.

God is calling us to enlarge our perspective and open our hearts from the vantage point of heaven and begin to see through the eyes of Christ. Then we will start to see a whole new world that will change our lives. It will change the way you live. Trials and hard times will take on a genuine new meaning. Our sense of purpose will be restored. Knowing

Say It Again

that God is in control and has a plan for our lives will bring us hope.

> *2 Corinthians 4:18: "So we fix our eyes not on what is seen, but on what is seen. For what is seen is temporary, but what is unseen is eternal."*

> *Isaiah 55:8-9: "For my thoughts are not your thoughts, neither are your ways my ways," declares the Lord. As the heavens are higher than the earth, so are my ways higher than your ways and my thoughts than your thoughts."*

I lived in Leesburg, Georgia, while we were raising our two beautiful children. For seven years, we lived downtown in a laid-back country setting. Our little city had two parades every year. We had a Homecoming and a Christmas parade. The great thing about that was the parade on Main Street, where I lived. That means I didn't have to fight traffic to get there. My family just walked out the front door and stood by our front gate. The entire parade would pass right by, and we could see every float. The crowds grew, and more people gathered in front of our house. Then my kids began to complain that they couldn't see. So they squeezed their heads through the crowd to glimpse each float as they drove by. They became frustrated and irritated, but I had a great idea. So, I grabbed the kids and went back inside the house. They were upset because they were missing the parade. Then we went upstairs to the front bedroom and threw open the window overlooking the parade. To their surprise, they could see so much more. Instead of seeing want was in front of them. They could see multiple floats, plus all the people standing up and down the street. They enjoyed this new perspective.

Life can be confusing. It can be challenging at times. You may feel like you are walking in circles. You may need to gain a new perspective or rise above the crowd. You have been frustrated and irritated with those around you. I want to encourage you to take a look from God's perspective. You may need to change the place where you are standing. But it will be worth the effort. Know this; He sees your beginning and your end. He understands where we are, and He is willing to give us understanding.

> *Jeremiah 29:11-13: "For I know the plans I have for you,' declares the Lord. 'plans to prosper you and not to harm you, plans to give you hope and a future. Then you will call upon me and come and pray to me, and I will listen to you. You will seek me and find me when you seek me with all your heart."*

Take another look, Church. Take time to pray and to seek His face. It may change how you see people and how you live life.

-11-
Committed

Romans 12:1-2: "Therefore, I urge you, brothers, in view of God's mercy, to offer your bodies as living sacrifices, holy and pleasing to God this is your spiritual act of worship. Do not conform any longer to the pattern of this world, but be transformed by the renewing of your mind. Then you will be able to test and approve what God's will is his good, pleasing, and perfect will."

Why do you suppose there are so many churches in America, yet we are not making the moral and spiritual impact we should? Why do thousands of churches have more empty pews than full on Sunday morning? If we believe there is a heaven and a hell, why do we keep quiet about the Gospel of Jesus Christ? Why do so many pastors plead for members to get involved in church ministry?

There is one standard answer to all those questions. The answer is this: We, as Christians, have decided about Jesus but never committed to Him. In other words: Some realized they didn't want to go to hell and preferred to spend eternity in a much more comfortable place called heaven. So, they decided to receive Jesus Christ as their personal Savior.

In other words, every person who gets married decides to speak their vows to each other. They exchange rings, and then they kiss each other. They decided to marry. Committing means turning something over to someone—yielding to them, surrendering to them, and placing your life at their disposal. When a man and a woman commit to marriage, they testify to the world that they have abandoned themselves. They turn their back on all others till death do us part. That's commitment. The woman is saying: I am entrusting my life to my husband. She even changed her last name. The man says: I'm willing to surrender myself to you and promise to care for his wife. He promises to provide for her and love her forever. That's commitment.

Commitment to God means the same thing. It's saying to God: I yield myself to you. I surrender all, and I am placing my life at your disposal. I am abandoning myself to live for you. Perhaps, you have been a Christian for forty years, but since you have been saved, has there been a time when you committed your entire life to Jesus? I am talking about a commitment without reservation and hesitation. There is no such thing as partial obedience. As God works in our lives, He keeps bringing us to a deeper level of commitment. Do we stay grounded and safe to what is familiar, or do we take off and fly in our faith?

Being committed to Jesus Christ is serious business. We must commit to Him fully to reach the maxim of our potential in Him. We will never find true contentment, true joy, or true peace. Genuine commitment is saying to the Lord, "I am climbing on the altar of the Lord. Here I am, God! I am laying down my life to You." Look at what Isaiah said in Isaiah 6:8:

"Here am I. Send me!"

Isaiah was all in. He was holding nothing back. Are we committed to Him with no strings attached? Have you ever prayed, "Lord, whatever you want, I am yours, or wherever you want me to go, I will go?" Why are we so scared to fully commit ourselves to the Lord? Do we believe that God wants His very best for us? Look at what Paul is writing to the people in Corinth in 2 Corinthians 6:14-18:

> *"Do not be yoked together with unbelievers. For what do righteousness and wickedness have in common? Or what fellowship can light have with darkness? What harmony is there between Christ and Belial? What does a believer have in common with an unbeliever? What agreement is there between the temple of God and idols? For we are the temple of the living God. As God has said, 'I will live with them and walk among them, and I will be their God, and they will be my people.' 'Therefore come out from them and be separate, says the Lord. Touch no unclean thing, and I will receive you.' 'I will be a Father to you, and you will be my sons and daughters, says the Lord Almighty.'"*

Sometimes, our commitment wavers because we spend too much time flirting with the worldly desires around us. Commitment to the Lord Jesus means separating ourselves from ungodly passion, worldly lust, and sinful pride. It means leaving the lust of the flesh, the lust of the eyes, and running to the presence of the Father.

> *1 John 2:15-17: "Do not love the world or anything in the world. If anyone loves the world, the love of the Father is not in him. For everything in the world-the craving of sinful man, the lust of his eyes, and the boasting of what he has and does, comes not from the Father but from the world. The world and its desires pass away, but the man who does the will of God lives forever."*

I hate to say it, but we have become a people of comfort and convenience. We have grown up with a Burger King kind of faith. It's a faith where we want it our way. I think we are all guilty at some time or another when we say, "Lord, I will serve you if it is within a desirable driving distance." "Lord, I surrender all, but I can't move and leave my family and friends behind." Think about it, how many of us sit in the same seat every single Sunday? How many of us have sat in that same seat for twenty years? Lord, help the person who dares to sit in our seats. We love comfort. We love convenience. We tend to pick and choose what we commit to the Lord. But our Heavenly Father held nothing back from us. He gave His very best! He gave us His only Son to die on an old rugged cross. Every drop of Jesus' precious blood was poured out for us. Jesus held nothing back. He didn't choose what was comfortable or convenient. He was fully committed to the Father's plan for His life.

I know this will not be a desirable message, but the truth needs to be told. God rarely calls His Church to the easy life. I can probably get a couple of 'amens' with that statement. First, have you ever noticed that the Bible isn't a book of convenience? The Word of God speaks about sacrifice, going the extra mile, enduring hardships, and overcoming obstacles.

I am not a pilot and don't know much about flying, but I love flying on planes. My favorite part of the flight is the take-off. As we approach our assigned runway, I always ensure my window is open to see outside the plane. Then the Captain waits for the final clearance to take off. When he receives that final ok, he turns up the engines, and the plane moves forward. As the aircraft builds up speed, you can feel its power, and the runway gets shorter and shorter. The plane is now at full speed, and we are approaching the point

Say It Again

where the pilot has to decide whether I stay grounded or commit to the air. When we cross that line, that pilot is dedicated to the air, or the plane will crash. However, I still enjoy that feeling when the aircraft leaves the ground, and we soar into the sky.

If we are committed to the Lord Jesus, we must be determined to stop setting on our runway and revving up our engines. We must be determined to fly, but flying requires committing to the Lord Jesus. Unfortunately, so many Christians have sat so long on the runway of the Church that we have become lazy and content. Fear of the unknown has grounded you and those around you, and we haven't experienced the power of lift-off.

Jesus died for you and me. He came to this earth because He loved us, and He wanted to be obedient to the plans of the Heavenly Father. So, he lived the perfect life without sin and became God's perfect, spotless Lamb. Jesus faced all the pain, suffering, and humiliation. In other words, He took our place and paid the price we should have paid. Jesus willingly died on an old rugged cross, but three days later, our Lord overcame sin and death and came out of that grave. The good news is that He is alive and well today and reigns on my heart's throne. Because of the truth, I am free! I am made whole! I am a child of Almighty God! Because of that truth, I can commit to heading down that spiritual airstrip, taking off, and enjoying the ride of a lifetime.

I want to encourage you to relinquish all claims to your life. Lay aside the quest for the easy road and the bogus brand of Christianity that doesn't call for commitment. So, what are you waiting on? Commit to the air and get ready to fly in Christ. A new adventure awaits you, a new way of living when we finally surrender and commit our entire life to Jesus. So take off; it's time to fly. Open up the shade of the window, and look at the power of God as you leave the ground. "Thank you, Lord Jesus!"

-12-
Compassion

God has a plan for our lives. That plan is to have an intimate love relationship with us. From the beginning of time, God created us for fellowship. So God created Adam and Eve, and they walked in close fellowship with the Lord. Look at what happened when Satan approached Eve in the beautiful garden of Eden.

> *Genesis 3:1-6: "Now the serpent was more crafty than any of the wild animals the Lord God had made. He said to the woman, 'Did God really say, 'You must not eat from any tree in the Garden?' The woman said to the serpent, 'We may eat fruit from the tree in the garden, but God did say, 'You must not eat fruit from the tree that is in the middle of the garden, and you must not touch it, or you will die.' 'You will not surely die,' the serpent said to the woman. 'For God knows that when you eat of it your eyes will be opened, and you will be like God, knowing good and evil.' When the woman saw that the fruit of the tree was good for food and pleasing to the eye, and also desirable for gaining wisdom, she took some and ate it. She also gave some to her husband, who was with her, and he ate it."*

They disobeyed God, and here is where sin entered this world. You see, God is a holy God and cannot have anything to do with sin. That sin separated us from the God of all creation. But God made a way to restore us to a right relationship with Him. He sent His Son Jesus to be born of a virgin. He lived a sinless life and became God's perfect Lamb. Jesus willingly laid down His life on the cross. He suffered, bled, and died a criminal's death. But three days later, Jesus overcame sin and death and is sitting at the right hand of the Lord.

As believers in Jesus Christ, we need to place our right foot on the cross of Christ. But we must also put our left foot on the empty grave and stand firm on our Christian faith. Because of this truth, I can face tomorrow. Because of this truth, I experience life, peace, joy, and happiness, and I have a promise of eternal life. "Thank you, Jesus!"

But here is the question I want to ask you. Where would you be without Jesus? Think about that for a few minutes. How will you respond? The second question I want to ask you is this: Do you believe in the Gospel of Jesus Christ? If you believe in the Gospel of Jesus Christ, God will fill you with compassion. That compassion will lead you to a new life in Jesus. So, I want to share three points with those born-again believers in Jesus Christ.

1. If you believe in the Gospel of Jesus, then simple compassion will compel us to share it.

Matthew 20:29-34: "As Jesus and his disciples were leaving Jericho, a large crowd followed him. Two blind men were sitting by the roadside, and when they heard that Jesus was going by, they shouted, 'Son of David, have mercy on us!' The crowd rebuked them and told them to be quiet, but they shouted all the louder, 'Lord, Son of David, have mercy on us!' Jesus stopped and called them. 'What do you want me to do for you?' he asked. 'Lord,' they answered, 'we want our sight.' Jesus had compassion on them and

Say It Again

touched their eyes. Immediately they received their sight and followed him."

Thinking about the lostness of this world is overwhelming. Sometimes, I feel so small, but I know I have to do something. Jesus was compassionate and cared deeply about those he encountered in his daily walk of life. I am sure Jesus' days were wide open, and he had places to be and people to speak with. While Jesus was leaving Jericho, two blind men cried to Him to get His attention. The crowd rebuked them, but that didn't stop them from calling out to Jesus. They were in desperate need and needed a healing touch from the world's Savior. I love what happened. Next, scripture tells us that Jesus stopped! He stopped because He had compassion for them. Then Jesus touched their eyes and restored their sight.

This world is in desperate need of healing. This world is screaming out because people need someone to care. But do we have the kind of compassion that Jesus possessed? Do we stop meeting the needs of the people around us? "Lord, give us the heart to love other people to you. Fill us to overflow with love, kindness, gentleness, and joy. Do we care enough to share our faith with those spiritually blind and covered with pain and regrets? Simple compassion compels us to stop and see those in need and hurting. We must care enough to share Jesus and what He has done for us.

We talk about evangelism and sharing our faith in the strangest ways. Many say, "Until the Holy Spirit prompts me, I will not share my faith." How crazy is that? Imagine this if you can. You and I took a walk together, and we came to a railroad crossing and saw an unconscious boy lying on the tracks. We heard the train screaming down the tracks as we noticed the boy. What do you do? Do you stop and pray and ask God what to do? No! You pick the boy up off the tracks and take him to the hospital and get him some help. Simple compassion would compel us to pick that boy up and save him from the upcoming train.

Care enough to slow down from your fast-paced life. When God provides an opportunity to share the Gospel of Jesus, stop and share His goodness. Simple compassion will compel us to share.

2. We owe the Gospel to others.

Let that sink in. We owe the gospel to our friends at work. We owe the gospel to the neighbors around us. We owe the gospel to the people whom we do not like. The greatest injustice in the Church happens when those of us who know the gospel do not share it with those who don't know Jesus.

> *Matthew 28:18-20: "Then Jesus came to them and said, 'All authority in heaven and on earth has been given to me. Therefore go and make disciples of all nations, baptizing them in the Father and of the Son and of the Holy Spirit, and teaching them to obey everything I have commanded you. And surely I am with you always, to the very end of the age."*

The question is no longer if you are called, only where and how.

> *2 Peter 3:9: "The Lord is not slow in keeping his promise, as some understand slowness. He is patient with you, not wanting anyone to perish, but everyone to come to repentance."*

Say It Again

He desires that all come to repentance. His will for the lost helps me to understand His will for my life. Where God sends us is up to Him, but whether He called us to share has already been settled. Church, we can't be satisfied and content. God is calling His Church to rise up. We are called to be a light in a dark and dying world. We are called to stand on God's Word and proclaim His truth. We are called to pray bold prayers and stand our ground. We are called to share our stories and tell others what a difference Jesus has made in our lives. But does the attitude of our hearts line up with what we confess with our mouths?

> *Romans 9:1-4: "I speak the truth in Christ, I am not lying, my conscience confirms it in the Holy Spirit. I have great sorrow and unceasing anguish in my heart. For I could wish that I myself were cursed and cut off from Christ for the sake of my brothers, those of my own race, the people of Israel."*

Paul had a burden for the people of Israel to know Christ. Think about what Paul was saying. He was willing to be cut off from Christ for Israel to find salvation. His heart was broken over the lostness of Israel. That brings me to a question I want you to ponder. Has God's love given you this kind of compassion for the people around you? Sharing the gospel isn't always easy; different fears and doubts flood our minds. Sharing our faith isn't about knowing the complexities of theology or having all the correct answers. But it is about understanding that Jesus loves us and that He came to set us free from sin. He saved us from judgment by paying our sin debt and overcoming death. He desires that all men will come to know Him through an intimate personal love relationship. Through Jesus, we all can experience freedom, love, and His marvelous grace. We owe the gospel to others!

3. We can't experience Jesus and remain silent.

I have to ask you again, where would you be without Jesus? Think about it; thousands and thousands of people need to hear the message of Jesus. Think about all the people you encounter daily that are empty, hurting, and depressed. Our mission field is in our homes, schools, grocery stores, and the ball fields near our homes. If you are in Christ, you have a gift that needs to be given away. His name is Jesus.

> *Romans 10:14-17: "How, then, can they call on the one they have not believed in? And how can they believe in the one who they have not heard? And how can they hear without someone preaching to them? And how can they preach unless they are sent? As it is written, 'How beautiful are the feet of those who bring good news?'"*

Our greatest example gives us a great go-by when sharing our faith. Take a look at Matthew 9:35-38:

> *"Jesus went through all the towns and villages, teaching in their synagogues, preaching the good news of the kingdom, and healing every disease and sickness. When he saw the crowds, he had compassion on them because they were harassed and helpless, like a sheep without a shepherd. Then he told his disciples, "The harvest is plentiful but the workers are few. Ask the Lord of the harvest, therefore, to send out workers into his harvest field."*

Say It Again

We cannot remain silent, Church! We must follow the example that Christ has given us here in Matthew chapter nine. Jesus got outside of the four walls of the church building. He got involved in people's lives and met the needs of those around Him. Jesus was full of compassion, and He cared deeply about people. Then He calls for us, His Church, to do the same. This world needs to hear about the saving grace of Jesus!

"Empty us, O God, of selfishness and pride. Then fill us with your love and compassion to the point where we spill Jesus everywhere we go. Then, let's put compassion into action. To God be the glory!"

-13-
Where's the Zeal?

One of my favorite commercials had two old ladies looking at a hamburger on a table. The two older ladies inspected the hamburger and looked it over well. Then one of the ladies picked up the hamburger and asked, "Where's the beef?" Yes, you guessed it. It was a Wendy's commercial from way back. I want to start chapter thirteen with a similar question to get your mind in gear. So my question to you is this: Where is the zeal? In other words, where is the passion? Did you wake up excited about meeting with the God of the universe this morning? Are you bubbling over with joy and can't wipe your smile off your face? Where is our zeal for the Lord? Where is our passion for the things of God? What consumes our thoughts? What motivates us? What gets us excited? What do we dream about?

> *John 16:12-15: "I have much more to say to you, more than you can now bear. But when he, the Spirit of truth, comes, he will guide you into all truth. He will not speak on his own; he will speak only what he hears, and he will tell you what is yet to come. He will bring glory to me by taking from what is mine and making it known to you. All that belongs to the Father is mine. That is why I said the Spirit will take from what is mine and make it known to you."*

We have an opportunity every morning to sit down to a spiritual feast. God's buffet table and it is all you eat! But for some reason, we settled for a spiritual stale bologna sandwich. Taste and see that the Lord is good. Again I ask, "Where is our passion for God's Holy Word?" Take time to feast on God's best and dig deep into the truths God wants to show us daily. Allow the Holy Spirit inside of you to share fresh bread from the very heart of God.

I want to give you three things we need to help us raise our zeal levels. First, I want to provide you with a push to get your passion level jump-started. There are many ways to do this, but these three steps have helped me the most. There is no magic formula or complex process, but easy everyday stuff that we as believers must faithfully walk out daily. So hold on, and let's jump into His Word and see what the Lord gives us.

1. Prayer has to be a priority in our life.

To me, this is where zeal is born. Prayer is talking and listening to God. It's a continual conversation with the Savior of the world. Have you ever noticed that the more one hangs out with another person, the more one becomes like the other? My wife and I have been married for thirty-seven years, which is a long time. What is so scary, the longer we are together, the more we become like each other. We know what each other is thinking and can sometimes finish each other's sentences. In other words, the more time you sit in the presence of the Lord in prayer, the more you can become like Him.

How can we get zeal?

John 16:24: "Until now you have not asked for anything in my name. Ask and you will receive, and your joy will be complete."

To receive zeal, start by asking God for it. Tell Him exactly where you are in your journey of life. Does He already know? Of course, but He wants to hear from us. Be honest with God and talk to Him like you would speak to your closest friends. You don't have to enter your King James language for God to understand you. Ask Him to fill you with passion for the things of God and ask that the people see a difference in you. Pray it. Mean it. Then believe it.

> 2 Chronicles 7:14: "If my people who are called by my name, will humble themselves and pray and seek my face and turn from their wicked ways, then I will hear from heaven and will forgive their sins and will heal their land."

"Lord, hear our prayers today. Light a fire under Your Church and fill us will zeal for You. Motivate us. Inspire us and grow us, Lord." I want to encourage you to lift this simple prayer to the Lord and not be scared to pray it more than once. The great thing about zeal is that it is contagious. Make sure to block out times during the day to listen and talk with your Heavenly Father. Don't hesitate to pray for passion.

2. Our priorities have to be in line.

> Matthew 6:33: "But seek first his kingdom and his righteousness, and all these things will be given to you as well."

Why are worry and stress so evident in our society today? Why do so many people seem so tired and worn out? It's because we are running after the things of this world more than we are running after the things of God. I know that is a straightforward answer, but that is the truth. So let me ask you another question, what causes more problems in marriage than anything else? Yes, it is financial debt. We see things we desire and think we must have that immediately to be happy. So we spend so much more time at work trying to pay for it with our overtime pay, or we put it on our credit card. Then debt begins to build up. Then two years later, we wondered how we got into this financial debt. It started because our priorities did line up with God's heart.

Has God taken a back seat, or have other things become more important to you than your relationship with the Lord? So often, we are so focused on material possessions that we don't have and spend so much time figuring out how to get them; God's time is squeezed out. When our priorities are out of line, we can't see the blessings of God. We can't recognize how God is working around us. Then we are missing out on the best that God has to offer.

Let me ask you a few more questions to get you to think. What is most important to you? What do you spend the majority of your day doing? What is your purpose in life? Are you fulfilling your purpose? Are you making a difference in the lives of people around you? I challenge you to slow down enough to answer these questions and then sit down with a friend and discuss it. I encourage you to keep the main thing the main thing. The main thing is enjoying a passionate love relationship with the Heavenly Father. If we keep Him first, everything else seems to fall in place.

3. Be willing to give Him everything. "Total Surrender"

You may say you can handle praying more and place God as your first priority, but being totally surrendered may be too much. So again, look at the words of Jesus in Matthew 4:18-20:

> *"As Jesus was walking beside the Sea of Galilee, he saw two brothers, Simon called Peter, and his brother Andrew. They were casting a net into the lake, for they were fishermen. 'Come, follow me." Jesus said, 'And I will make you fishers of men.' At once they left their nets and followed him."*

These men heard the voice of Jesus and obeyed His voice. They were sold out. In other words, they were all in. They left their nets behind. They left everything familiar and everything they held dear and followed Jesus' instructions. There was no hesitation; they gladly followed Him. Think about how hard that had to be for these fishermen. Fishing was the only thing they knew to earn a living. Can you imagine the questions they must have had when Jesus was talking with them? Look at Matthew 16:24-25:

> *"Then Jesus said to his disciples, 'If anyone would come after me, he must deny himself and take up his cross and follow me. For whoever wants to save his life will lose it, but whoever loses his life for me will find it.'"*

"I will follow You no matter the cost." Can you say that to your Heavenly Father today? What's holding you back? What's stopping you from going all in? I know it will not be easy, but neither was leaving heaven to come to earth and die on a rugged cross. I want to challenge you to pray a prayer I wrote in my book called Surrendered. If you dare, please pray this prayer out loud:

Say It Again

"Father, in the name of Jesus, I place my body, soul, spirit, and entire being into your hands. I now ask that You place me in Your perfect will and plan for my life. Father, from this moment on, I will choose to stay fully surrendered to You for all the days of my life, and I allow You to lead and direct my life in the direction that You will want it to go in. I am stepping into Your yoke, and I am trusting You fully. I am following Your lead, Father."

Church, where is our passion? Where is our zeal for Christ? Biblical zeal is found in fervent prayer. It's found in placing God first in everything we do and in totally surrendering our entire life to the call of Jesus. I pray against spiritual contentment that slips into the back doors of our lives. Church, we all have a job to tell the world about the amazing love of a Holy God that loved us so much that He sent His Son to die on the cross. We are called to be a lighthouse that shines in the darkness and rescues people from the dangers of the enemy.

Where's the love? Where's the grace? Where's the mercy? Be full of passion and zeal and share with this world what God has done for us. To God be the glory forever and ever.

-14-
Doing Life Together

We all need relationships. It is so much fun to hang out and have a good time with your closest friends. Whether you go out to eat or have them over to the house, having someone to talk to or taking a long trip to keep you awake while driving is great. But relationships can also be challenging. The church is not exempt from those challenges. I believe every church has what I call E.G.R.s. Those are the people where extra grace is required. You know what I am talking about. Maybe you have been burned in the past, or perhaps you have been betrayed by a friend, and now you believe that friends are overrated. If you live long enough, you will experience some really good times with friends and cherish those memories, but you will also have some friends that break your heart. So with all that being said, are you doing life together with someone, or are you doing life alone?

God has a plan for relationships, and He gave us Jesus to give us an excellent example of how to treat the people around us. Take time now and think about all the friends in your life. Whom do you pull into your inner circle? Which friends do you keep at a distance? Who do you go to when you need to discuss something very personal? How about these questions: Are you a good friend? Is there an area in your life where there needs to be personal growth? Do you build up or tear down those around you? When it comes down to it, we all have room to become better friends and learn how to live with those whom God has surrounded us with. There are three things Jesus did well when doing life with His friends.

Say It Again

1. Jesus gained the Father's heart for people.

Think about it: Jesus had his small group and His E.G.Rs. Look at the life of Peter; he was always talking. He tended to say what was on his mind and always had an opinion. Thomas was the doubter and always questioned the decisions that were being made. Can you imagine what it was like to have ex-tax collectors in your inner circle?

Even Jesus experienced one of His closest friends stab Him in the back and betray Him. Jesus was saying to His friends, let's do life together. In other words, Jesus poured His life into this group of men. They spent so much time with each other and knew each other like the back of their hands. Despite their differences, they turned the world upside down.

> *Acts 2:42-47: "They devoted themselves to the apostles teaching and to the fellowship, to the breaking of bread and to prayer. Everyone was filled with awe, and many wonders and miraculous signs were done by the apostles. All the believers were together and had everything in common. Selling their possessions and goods, they gave to anyone as he had need. Every day they continued to meet together in the temple courts; they broke bread in their homes and ate together with glad and sincere hearts, praising God and enjoying the favor of all the people. And the Lord added to their number daily those who were being saved."*

Doesn't that sound like something you would like to be involved with? It sounds like they were having the time of their life. They were getting together, eating, and having a great time. If that wasn't enough, they were praying up a storm, and lives were being changed for the glory of God. They gathered together to worship in homes and the temple courts. God has created us to have long-lasting, life-changing relationships. If we choose a life of isolation, I guarantee you will not live a life that impacts others. God calls us to step out in faith and do life together. We all need time together to receive godly teaching from the Word of God. We require that fellowship time with friends and family. We also need that time to pray as a group and share life's ups and downs. Not only can someone touch your life, but you can also touch someone. Catch the vision that the Father had for building relationships.

2. Jesus encountered the power of God in His relationships.

Life transformation took place when they all got together. Scripture tells us they were filled with awe; the apostles did many wonders and miraculous signs and had an incredible unity spirit. Everyone was also shown accountability, support, encouragement, and genuine love. God's presence and power were there and made a difference in the lives of those who attended. We need each other!

The enemy aims to isolate and pick off as many as possible. He wants to separate you from the body of Christ and then tear you apart from your purpose and passion. He wants to come and try to steal the joy of your salvation and distract you from your gaze on the Savior of the world.

3. Jesus embraced the purpose of God in His small group of friends.

Say It Again

God's ultimate goal for us is to love Him with all our heart, mind, soul, and strength. And to love our neighbor as ourselves. There is no better place to experience this than in a small group with other believers in Christ. God uses His Church to encourage each other when times get hard, or we are going through a difficult situation. He places people in your life who can speak words of encouragement or words of instruction, and even correction.

Over the years, I have seen so many believers fall away from the Church, and they push God to the backside of their priorities. They started so well, and they were excited about their newfound relationship with the Lord, but they never seemed to get connected with other believers for one reason or another. They enjoyed their time of worship in the church setting but never got associated with a small group setting. Over time, with no accountability, they found other things to do with their time on Sunday.

> *Hebrews 10:21-25: "Since we have a great priest over the house of God, let us draw near to God with a sincere heart in full assurance of faith, having our hearts sprinkled to cleanse us from a guilty conscience and having our bodies washed with pure water. Let us hold unswervingly to the hope we profess, for he who promised is faithful. And let us consider how we may spur one another on toward love and good deeds. Let us not give up meeting together, as some are in the habit of doing, but let us encourage one another, and all the more as you see the Day approaching."*

What an encouraging word to the Church of Jesus Christ from the writer of Hebrews. He sends us a challenge to draw near to God sincerely and hold on to the hope we profess. Grip it tight, and don't let go for any reason. Ensure you are involved with a group of believers digging into God's Word. Doing life together also involves us spurring each other towards the love of God and good deeds. It is always good to have encouragement and sometimes a kick in the pants to keep us going. Do you have that kind of relationship you can count on?

> Proverbs 18:24: "A man of many companions may come to ruin, but there is a friend who sticks closer than a brother."

> Proverbs 27:17: "As iron sharpens, so one man sharpens another."

We all have a massive need for an authentic community. Authentic community connects with a group of believers with a sense of community, accountability, and belonging. The by-product of genuine community is spiritual growth. Lives will be changed when we decide to do life together. Don't be that 'Lone-ranger-Christian' and try to do everything yourself. Small groups do work and are needed if we want the Church to continue to grow. Meeting in small groups was Jesus' design to nurture and equip the Church. Step out of that comfort zone, and let's spur each other on in the name of our Lord Jesus!

-15-
Ready, Set, Go

Matthew 28:18-19: "Then Jesus came to them and said, 'All authority in heaven and on earth has been given to me. Therefore go and make disciples of all nations, baptizing them in the name of the Father and of the Son and of the Holy Spirit, and teaching them to obey everything I have commanded you. And surely I am with you always, to the very end of the age."

What do we believe? Do we believe that Jesus is the Son of God? Do we believe that He is the light of the world? Do we think Jesus is the King of kings and the Lord of lords? Do we believe He is the source of hope, joy, and true happiness? Do we believe that our Lord is in control? Do we think He can make a difference in people's hearts? So then, why is the Church so quiet? Why aren't we shouting it from the rooftops?

Church, we have been quiet long enough! It is time to take it off cruise control and for the Church of Jesus Christ to sound the alarm. I pray that God will open our spiritual eyes to see as He sees. "Shake us up, Lord, disturb us and our busy schedules. Stir up in us a spirit of urgency, a spirit of compassion, and a fresh spirit of love within Your Church.

The Heavenly Father has issued a command here in Matthew twenty-eight. Notice something; this is not known as the Great Suggestion. Instead, it is called the Great Commission. He is calling us to go. We have done enough sitting; we are called to go into a lost and dying world and love people. We are to build relationships and serve the people. We are called to go and give away His love to those who are hurting, lost, and those who are empty and searching for purpose in life.

Have you ever stopped and taken a good look at the world that we are living in? Have you stopped and looked at your local newscast and seen all the chaos that is going on all around us? Broken homes are at an all-time high. Sickness and disease tear this world apart in several ways. Satan is on the attack, and He will not ease up. He is determined to cause as much destruction as possible before being handcuffed and thrown into hell forever. In the meantime, he is doing everything he can to cause us grief.

Church, it is time to engage our hearts and our hands. It is time to put into action what we believe. It's time to get our hands dirty and love people to Jesus Christ. Again, look at the example that Jesus gave us in Matthew 9:35-36:

> *"Jesus went through all the towns and villages, teaching in their synagogues, preaching the good news of the kingdom, and healing every disease and sickness. When he saw the crowds, he had compassion on them, because they were harassed and helpless, like sheep without a shepherd."*

Jesus went outside the four walls of the church building and loved on people. He was full of compassion, and He felt their pain and suffering. But look at what Jesus has to say to us in Matthew 9:37-38:

> *"The harvest is plentiful but the workers are few. Ask the Lord of the harvest, therefore, to send out workers into his harvest field."*

Say It Again

Jesus is calling us to a grander vision of living. Saying yes to God's grander vision of living is saying yes to people. I encourage you to slow down long enough to see what is eternal and temporary. What are you investing in that will fade away and crumble one day? Are you investing in people's souls who will spend eternity in hell or heaven? We need to see that Jesus loved people. He genuinely cared for people most genuinely.

Jesus is calling the world to Himself. He calls them to come as they are, for the Kingdom of God is open to them. A grander vision of living is looking through the eyes of Christ and seeing people who do not know Jesus and seeing their potential once they receive God's love and power. What would happen in our churches if we were passionate about carrying out the Great Commission? What would happen in our cities and our prisons all over the country if the Church of the living God would put on the eyes of Christ and share our testimony? Can you imagine how our school systems would be different?

I must confess I love seeing born-again believers catching the vision of reaching out to people for Christ. I especially enjoy hearing that one of them has led someone to Christ for the first time. But even more than this, I love seeing a few infectious Christians spread the germ to others in their fellowship. Who in turn pass it on to more people until an evangelistic epidemic erupts throughout the church. If God can so effectively use one contagious Christian, what will happen when the whole church becomes contagious? When that happens, we are talking about an explosive spiritual impact throughout the entire community.

I don't have to tell you that most churches aren't like that yet. Far too many times, churches are trying to retain their membership, meet the budget, and maintain the status quo, and they have no real vision for reaching the lost. The truth is, dying churches are focused on membership. When the church is inwardly focused, they become self-serving and ask what it does for them. In that case, the church is irrelevant.

> *Matthew 16:13-18: "When Jesus came to the region of Caesarea Philippi, he asked his disciples, 'Who do people say the Son of Man is?' They replied, 'Some say John the Baptist; others say Elijah; and still others, Jeremiah or one of the prophets.' 'But what about you?' he asked. 'Who do you say I am?' Simon Peter answered, 'You are the Christ, the Son of the living God.' Jesus replied, 'Blessed are you, Simon son of Jonah, for this was not revealed to you by man but by my Father in heaven. And I tell you that you are Peter, and on this rock, I will build my church, and the gates of Hades will not overcome it.'"*

Jesus was talking about building a Church that the gates of hell couldn't overcome. So you see, His vision of the Church would be active and on the move. His Church would be dynamic and all about life change. It will be an expanding force to be reckoned with. Jesus's mission for the Church was to rescue, redeem, and recruit people mired in sin. We have a tremendous job ahead of us and must be on guard against complacency. People need the Lord, and God has given us the commission to share the Truth of Jesus with this lost and dying world.

Sharing Christ can be as simple as a walk across a room; just a few ordinary Spirit-guided steps can have a life-changing impact on the people around you. Think about it this way: Jesus walked out of heaven and wrapped Himself in human flesh. Then he stretched out His hands on a rugged cross to save us from our sins and the penalty of eternal damnation.

> *Romans 5:6-8: "And hope doesn't disappoint us because God has poured out his love into our hearts by the Holy Spirit, whom he has given us. You see, at just the right time, when we were still powerless, Christ died for the ungodly. Very rarely will anyone for a righteous man, though for a good man someone might possibly dare to die. But God demonstrates his own love for us in this: While we were still sinners, Christ died for us."*

What an amazing love! Christ extracted Himself from the ultimate circle of comfort to step across time and space to rescue us. Look at Paul's word in Philippians 2:6-8:

> *"Your attitude should be the same as that of Christ Jesus: Who being in the very nature of God, did not consider equality with God something to be grasped, but made himself nothing, taking the very nature of a servant, being made in human likeness. And being found in appearance as a man, he humbled himself and became obedient to death, even death on a cross!"*

Church, it is time to humble ourselves and rid ourselves of selfish pride. It is time to live by faith and not by sight. It is time to care for people and extend ourselves to our community. It is time to sow and water the seed of love with prayer. It is time to share the Good News of Jesus Christ and follow the nudging of the Holy Spirit in our lives. It is time to reach out and be a channel of God's great love. The time is now! Complacency has no place in the Church.

It's time to get to the starting line. So on your marks, get set, and go!

Say It Again

About The Author

I started in Student Ministry when I was twenty years old, and it has been my calling for nearly thirty years. My heart was for students to come to know Christ and to grow in their relationship with Him. I love to see God's light bulb fill their eyes and hearts, and I loved sharing the Gospel of Jesus with students whom everybody else said were a lost cause. My passion was to teach them about a relationship with the Lord and give them a real-life example of what it looked like to be walked out in everyday life. My time alone with God has always been my rock, fortress, and high tower. Spending time praying each morning, reading God's Word, and listening to His voice has changed my life forever. I love sharing with young believers who dare to dive deep into the river of God's love. It is so rewarding to invest in the life of other people, watching them go from the shallow end of faith and dive into the deep water of a love relationship with Jesus.

I had the privilege of pastoring two churches, a great blessing to my family and me. First, the Lord led us to plant a church in Leesburg, Georgia. It was a time of growth and a time of great joy. I loved preaching God's Word weekly and encouraging and loving families. We started with twelve people in our home one Sunday morning; a short time later, God opened the door to purchase a building on a couple of acres in Lee County. That church is still going strong and is known as Forrester Community Church. I also had the privilege of pastoring Salem Baptist Church in Worth County, Georgia. Salem is a small country church with a huge heart for God and its community. I was there briefly, but they have a special place in my heart.

Dennis L Taylor

Today, I serve as the Pastor of Sports and Recreation at Park Avenue in Titusville, Florida. Peter Lord was the founding pastor of Park Avenue Baptist Church. He was also the author of several well-known books such as Hearing God, Soul Care, 959 Plan, and many more. In addition, he was one of the greatest communicators of God's Word I have ever heard. I was honored to be discipled by this great man of God in 2004 as the Senior High Student Pastor. My role today at Park Avenue is to use sports and recreation to reach out to the community around us. As we develop relationships through sports, God opens the door to share our Jesus with them and their families. My hope, joy, and calling are to lead as many people as possible into a saving relationship with Jesus. Then encourage them to take those next steps to grow and mature in their faith.

In 2022 I wrote two devotional books, ***Fuel for Today Volumes One and Two***. I also penned the book ***The Total Package***, which deals with living a balanced life in Christ. My last book is ***Surrendered***, and my last devotional is ***He Fills My Cup***. I married Laura, my high school sweetheart, and we have been happily married for 36 years. The Lord has blessed us with two grown kids; Carsen serves in the Children's ministry at Passion City Church in Atlanta, Georgia. Mackenzie serves in the sports and recreation ministry at Warren Baptist Church in Augusta, Georgia.

Say It Again

More Books By Dennis L Taylor

1. **Fuel For Today:** A 6-Month Devotional Guide For Spiritual Growth And Encouragement
2. **The Total Package:** The Balanced Life
3. **Fuel For Today Volume 2:** A 3-Month Devotional Guide For Spiritual Growth And Encouragement.
4. **Surrendered:** From Stressed To Blessed; Your Best Life In Jesus' Easy Yoke
5. **He Fills My Cup:** A 90-Day Devotional To Refresh And Restore Your Soul; Drink From The Fountain.

www.ingramcontent.com/pod-product-compliance
Lightning Source LLC
Chambersburg PA
CBHW060841050426
42453CB00008B/784